# Art
## and the
# Gardener

*"The study of art is the most important study a garden designer can pursue."*

—MARCO POLO STUFANO,
GARDEN DESIGNER AND CURATOR

# Art
## and the
# Gardener

*Fine Painting as Inspiration for Garden Design*

# GORDON HAYWARD

**GIBBS SMITH**
TO ENRICH AND INSPIRE HUMANKIND
Salt Lake City | Charleston | Santa Fe | Santa Barbara

*To Mary, my muse*

First Edition
12 11 10 09 08          5 4 3 2 1

Published by
Gibbs Smith
P.O. Box 667
Layton, Utah 84041

Orders: 1.800.835.4993
www.gibbs-smith.com

Designed and produced by Rudy Ramos
Cover designed by Susan McClellan
Printed and bound in China

Library of Congress Cataloging-in-Publication Data

Hayward, Gordon.
  Art and the gardener : fine painting as inspiration for garden design / Gordon
Hayward. — 1st ed.
     p. cm.
  ISBN-13: 978-1-4236-0245-3
  ISBN-10: 1-4236-0245-5
  1.  Gardens—Design. 2.  Landscape design. 3.  Gardens in art.  I. Title.
  SB472.45.H39 2009
  712—dc22
                          2008020738

# Contents

Acknowledgments . . . . . . . . . . . . . . . . . . . . . . . . . . . . . . . . . . . . . . . .7

Introduction . . . . . . . . . . . . . . . . . . . . . . . . . . . . . . . . . . . . . . . . . . . .9

**Step I: Choose Your Style** . . . . . . . . . . . . . . . . . . . . . . . . . . . . . .17

    Romanticism . . . . . . . . . . . . . . . . . . . . . . . . . . . . . . . . . . . . . . . .18

    Classical Axial Design . . . . . . . . . . . . . . . . . . . . . . . . . . . . . . .22

    Impressionism . . . . . . . . . . . . . . . . . . . . . . . . . . . . . . . . . . . . .26

    Cubism . . . . . . . . . . . . . . . . . . . . . . . . . . . . . . . . . . . . . . . . . . .30

    Minimalism . . . . . . . . . . . . . . . . . . . . . . . . . . . . . . . . . . . . . . .34

    Abstract Expressionism . . . . . . . . . . . . . . . . . . . . . . . . . . . . . .38

    Pattern and Decoration . . . . . . . . . . . . . . . . . . . . . . . . . . . . . .42

    Contemporary . . . . . . . . . . . . . . . . . . . . . . . . . . . . . . . . . . . . .46

**Step II: The Relationship between House and Garden** . . . . . . . . . .53

    Garden as the Setting for the House . . . . . . . . . . . . . . . . . . .54

    Arriving at the Front Door . . . . . . . . . . . . . . . . . . . . . . . . . . .56

    View from the Front Door . . . . . . . . . . . . . . . . . . . . . . . . . . .58

    Views from Windows out into the Garden . . . . . . . . . . . . . .60

    A Terrace Relates Inside to Outside . . . . . . . . . . . . . . . . . . .62

    Sitting in the Garden . . . . . . . . . . . . . . . . . . . . . . . . . . . . . . .64

**Step III: Overall Composition** . . . . . . . . . . . . . . . . . . . . . . . . . . . .69

    The Process . . . . . . . . . . . . . . . . . . . . . . . . . . . . . . . . . . . . . . .69

    The Parts of a Whole Painting, a Whole Garden . . . . . . . . . . . .73

    Ten Methods of Composition for the Lansdscape Painter

        and Garden Designer . . . . . . . . . . . . . . . . . . . . . . . . . . . . .81

**Step IV: Design Principles** . . . . . . . . . . . . . . . . . . . . . . . . . . . . . .91

    Straight Paths . . . . . . . . . . . . . . . . . . . . . . . . . . . . . . . . . . . . .92

    The Tunnel . . . . . . . . . . . . . . . . . . . . . . . . . . . . . . . . . . . . . . .94

    Curving Paths . . . . . . . . . . . . . . . . . . . . . . . . . . . . . . . . . . . . .96

    Related Curves . . . . . . . . . . . . . . . . . . . . . . . . . . . . . . . . . . . .98

    Light: Dappled Shade . . . . . . . . . . . . . . . . . . . . . . . . . . . . . .100

    Focal Points . . . . . . . . . . . . . . . . . . . . . . . . . . . . . . . . . . . . .102

    Man-Made Structures Contrasting with Plants . . . . . . . . . . . .104

    The Outlook . . . . . . . . . . . . . . . . . . . . . . . . . . . . . . . . . . . . .106

    Contrasting Textures and Colors . . . . . . . . . . . . . . . . . . . . .108

    Creating Entrances, Transitions, and Edges . . . . . . . . . . . . . .110

**Step V: Roles Trees Play in the Garden** . . . . . . . . . . . . . . . . . . . . . .113

    Vertical Trees in a Horizontal Landscape . . . . . . . . . . . . . . . . . .114

    Creating Intimacy . . . . . . . . . . . . . . . . . . . . . . . . . . . . . . . . . . . .118

    Trees in Winter . . . . . . . . . . . . . . . . . . . . . . . . . . . . . . . . . . . . . .120

    The Orchard and Allée: Lines of Trees as Structural Elements . .122

    Low-Pruned Trees Compress Views under Them . . . . . . . . . . . .124

    Positive and Negative Space . . . . . . . . . . . . . . . . . . . . . . . . . . . .126

**Step VI: Color Harmony or Contrast** . . . . . . . . . . . . . . . . . . . . . .129

    The Gardener's Color Wheel . . . . . . . . . . . . . . . . . . . . . . . . . . . .130

    Color Schemes for the Garden . . . . . . . . . . . . . . . . . . . . . . . . . .133

    The Vocabulary of Color . . . . . . . . . . . . . . . . . . . . . . . . . . . . . . .133

    The Power of White . . . . . . . . . . . . . . . . . . . . . . . . . . . . . . . . . .133

    Green: Keeper of the Peace . . . . . . . . . . . . . . . . . . . . . . . . . . . . .134

    Grays and Gray Greens . . . . . . . . . . . . . . . . . . . . . . . . . . . . . . . .134

    Contrasting Colors in the Garden . . . . . . . . . . . . . . . . . . . . . . . .134

    Harmonious Colors in the Garden . . . . . . . . . . . . . . . . . . . . . . .135

    Color Combinations . . . . . . . . . . . . . . . . . . . . . . . . . . . . . . . . . .136

**Step VII: Bringing It All Together: Claude Monet's Life,**

**Garden, and Art** . . . . . . . . . . . . . . . . . . . . . . . . . . . . . . . . . . .151

**Floral Arrangements: Art in Bloom** . . . . . . . . . . . . . . . . . . . . . . .159

**Appendixes** . . . . . . . . . . . . . . . . . . . . . . . . . . . . . . . . . . . . . . . . . .162

**Index** . . . . . . . . . . . . . . . . . . . . . . . . . . . . . . . . . . . . . . . . . . . . . .170

# Acknowledgments

Over the last several years, as I worked on this book and its accompanying lecture, I spoke with many, many people about the crosscurrents between art and garden design. I want to thank those listed here for their willingness to listen and for their suggestions and comments. I especially want to thank artists Janet Fredericks and Leslie Parke as well as gardener and writer Sydney Eddison for their rich contributions in word and image. Without their help, this book would lack three layers of depth.

Peter and Caitlin Adair, friends who listen carefully and respond with substance

Kathy Anderson, artist working with Richard Schmid and The Putney Painters

Merry Armata of the Sterling and Francine Clark Art Institute, Williamstown, Massachusetts

Tom Armstrong, art administrator, garden maker and chairman of The Garden Conservancy

Jennifer Belt at Art Resources, New York City

Bob and Linda Boemig, sculptor and teacher, Brattleboro, Vermont

Peter and Siri Burki, art patrons, Easthampton, New York

Ralph Carpentier, artist, Easthampton, New York

Dan and Maggie Cassidy, friends who always offer insight

Carol, Heartstone Books, Putney, Vermont

Larry Carlson, artist and gardener, Sagaponock, New York

Guy Cohen, Campden Art Gallery, Chipping Campden, Gloucestershire, United Kingdom

Robert Dash, artist and gardener, Sagaponock, New York

Sydney Eddison, garden writer and gardener, Newtown, Connecticut

Marcel and Carolyn Elefant, art patrons, Montreal, Canada

Janet Fredericks, artist and illustrator, Lincoln, Vermont

Geoff Gaddis, poet, Putney, Vermont

Adam Glick and Denise Scruton, clients and friends

Hugo Grenville, artist, London, England

Mary Hayward, collaborator and my dear wife, Westminster West, Vermont

Peter Hayward, art collector, my brother, and orchardist, New Hartford, Connecticut

James Heffernan, English Department, Dartmouth College, Hanover, New Hampshire

Doug Hoerr, landscape architect, Chicago, Illinois

Nancy Hollis, librarian and researcher, Chestnut Hill, Massachusetts

Chris Kohan, Barge Art School, Long Island, New York

Rosemary Ladd and John Smith, artists, Putney, Vermont

Lorna Marsh, artist and gardener, Lake Forest, Illinois

Emily Mason, artist, New York, New York

Susan McClellan and her husband, photographer Richard Brown

Carol Mercer, garden designer, Easthampton, New York

Robert and Mimi Murley, clients and hosts, Lake Forest, Illinois

Hass Murphy and Diane Botnick, The Garden Conservancy, New York

John Nopper, photographer

Nancy Olson, researcher, friend, and teacher, Putney, Vermont

Leslie Parke, artist, Cambridge, New York

Anthony Paul, landscape architect, Surrey, England

Regina Quinn, slide librarian at the Sterling and Francine Clark Art Institute, Williamstown, Massachusetts

Victoria Jane Ream, art patron, author, and gardener, Salt Lake City, Utah

Cynthia Reeves and associates, Karen Mulcahy, and Azariah Aker at Reeves Contemporary Art Gallery, New York, New York, and Hanover, New Hampshire

Natasha and David Roderick Jones, Campden Bookshop, Chipping Campden, Gloucestershire, United Kingdom

Irene Roughton, Chrysler Museum of Art, Norfolk, Virginia

Roger and Mary Sandes, artists, Williamsville, Vermont

Richard Schmid and Nancy Guzik, artists, Putney, Vermont

George and Janet Scurria, art patrons, Cambridge, New York

Koo Shadler, artist, Putney, Vermont

Brian Sweetland, artist, East Rupert, Vermont

Nancy Thompson, art patron, Easton, Maryland

Doug Trump, artist, Marlboro, Vermont

Kit Ward, my agent

Nicole Wholean, David Rau, and Amy Lansing, Florence Griswold Museum, Old Lyme, Connecticut

"The real voyage of discovery consists not in seeking new landscapes, but in having new eyes."

——Marcel Proust (1871–1922), French writer

# INTRODUCTION

When designing your own garden, you set out to create an engaging, interesting place in which you, your family, and guests can live. As a novice in this sometimes daunting world of garden design, you may feel inadequate to the task. In this, my tenth book on garden design, I make a radical departure from my earlier approaches. Here I explore elements of visual language across two artistic disciplines—fine painting and garden design—in hopes that the remarkable crosscurrents between these two visual pursuits will help you design your new garden or simply appreciate your existing garden and those of others with greater acuity.

I have been exploring these crosscurrents since 1994 when the Museum of Fine Arts in Boston asked me to lecture on the relationship between art and the garden for their annual Art in Bloom program the following year. I spent a year looking for about forty pairs of images—one a garden, the other a painting—that would help me illustrate the correlation between these two disciplines. I have subsequently refined and developed this lecture over the past decade and have been surprised by the depth and breadth of the visual language we garden designers share with painters.

All my research gathers around seeing, around *taking the time* to see. Painters know how to see, and they have the skill and self-confidence to express on a canvas what they see by integrating color, line, form, balance, scale, and many other elements of visual expression into a harmonious whole that feels inevitable. Too often we look at paintings as objects, forgetting that the painting we so admire came out of, say, a painter named Childe Hassam, who visited gardener Celia Thaxter on the Isle of Shoals off the coast of Maine in the summer of 1892. What we see in Hassam's painting *In The Garden* (figure 1.3)—and all paintings—is a record of what he saw, how he felt, and what inspired him that summer day when Celia Thaxter agreed to stand in her garden for awhile as he painted.

At one point in my research I spoke with Marco Polo Stufano, the past head of gardens at Wave Hill, just north of Manhattan. He is one of the most accomplished gardeners and designers working in America today. He told me he studied art history in his undergraduate work and only got into gardening studies at the New York Botanic

Garden once he had completed his studies of art. He said, "The study of art is the most important study a garden designer can pursue. It's straightforward to memorize plant names; it's the eye you have to train. Studying art teaches you how to see."

Like Stufano, I turned to painters and their paintings over thirty years ago to teach me how to see. Since 1974, I have visited countless art museums across America, Europe, and Scandinavia, as well as Leningrad and Moscow. In preparation for writing this book, I've visited art galleries and spoken with painters across the country. I've also spoken with artists who are accomplished gardeners and gardeners who are artists.

As I travel the country designing residential gardens, I talk with homeowners who are often experiencing a crisis of confidence when it comes to expressing themselves in the form of their own gardens. They are hugely successful at designing and decorating their own homes or designing their own remarkable lives. Yet something happens when they stand at the doors of their homes, look out at the blank canvas that is their "yard" with feelings of inadequacy, and then call me or someone like me for assistance. The only difference between my clients and me is knowledge and perhaps a bit of intuition. And so in this book I want to explore that knowledge, that body of design elements that will energize and develop confidence in you so that you can create a garden, all the parts of which are in harmony with you and your house and site.

The principles of composition, color, form, line, texture, scale, and balance, among others—all those words you've heard about but barely understood—are, in fact, approachable, easily understood, and practical ideas. Principles are maps for action.

To bring these principles to life, to truly express yourself in your garden, you need to be clear about what it is you want to express. Is it your love of color, your need for order and linearity, your love of wild native plants in a wild setting, or perhaps something more personal? My wife, Mary, and I combined hints of our childhood with our love of informal familiar plantings within a linear firm structure to create our personal garden in Vermont, which follows sound design principles. (See *The Intimate Garden*.)

Mary grew up on a diversified farm in the Cotswold Hills of England. I grew up on an orchard in northwestern Connecticut. Over the past twenty-five years we have created a garden around our 230-year-old farmhouse that fuses Old England and New England gardening styles: beds and paths in straight English lines organized not only off the doors of the house but also a hundred-year-old shed, a gazebo, and an abandoned barn foundation. We then planted those linear beds in a very informal New England style, with plants that will flourish in our Vermont climate and feel right in this landscape of meadows and wooded hills. That is, we expressed our *selves.*

However, looking inside yourself and then simply expressing what you feel in the form of paths, plants, and ornaments may not lead to satisfying design. Uninformed self-expression—just doing whatever you feel like—does not necessarily satisfy those who visit your garden. You express, but others need to understand and feel what you are expressing. That's where the elements of visual language shared by painters and garden designers enter. In order to create a garden design that successfully communicates, that moves and challenges and engages, you need to know something about the principles of visual language.

In a lecture that painter René Magritte gave in 1938, he said that what we create—in our case, a garden—needs a design before viewers can properly understand its form, let alone derive pleasure from seeing it. The design puts the creator's intentions into three dimensions; when the viewer comprehends that message, communication opens up between viewer and artist. Magritte said that the broadly understood and shared "culture, convention and cognition" makes that design and thereby creates beauty others can appreciate.

A garden, like a painting, is an extension of the creator. Both make the inner person tangible; both make the soul, heart, and mind of the person external, warm, and able to be appreciated by others. In order to make a garden or a painting, you need to have faith in yourself that, with an understanding of widely accepted visual principles, others will see what you see as something worthy of attention. When you put yourself into what you create, something great artists do, when you combine your heart with your mind, in balance, you can create art. But—and this is a big but—you need to be willing to be vulnerable. After all, when you create a garden or a painting, you are saying, "I think this is beautiful." You are also saying, "This is me." The process of creating a garden, then, can also be both an act of self-discovery as well as self-expression.

A work of art, and this includes a well-designed and maintained garden, is found in the artist. A painting and a garden make all that is not tangible in him or her—soul, spirit, view of the world, personality—tangible. Art is culture made visible; art and gardens are the visible manifestations of inner being. This is a book, then, about seeing and about the principles of painting and garden design that will inform your conscious decisions as you develop your art in your garden. As Jim Nollman writes in *Why We Garden,* "We are visual creatures. Our visual sense is our most insistent sense; it rules our perception of the world and dominates our consciousness."

But I do need to acknowledge the differences between these two disciplines. Painting is two-dimensional; gardens are three-dimensional. Paintings are frozen in time; gardens exist in time. Hang a painting on a wall and it will last for decades, even centuries. Turn your back on a garden for even a few weeks and it begins to revert to nature, a process aided by the vagaries of weather and climate. Many would argue that gardening is not a visual art, in part because gardens are not lasting. Some would argue that gardening is not art but an artistic pursuit; it requires artistry, but it does not result in the creation of a work of art. The authors of the *Oxford English Dictionary* required just over nine thousand words to define the elusive term *art.* Here is their very first definition: "Skill; its display or application. Skill in doing anything as the result of knowledge and practice." Whether or not gardening is an

art or results in a work of art is an issue of semantics. Suffice it to say, this book is an exploration of how garden design is driven by many of the same elements of visual language used by painters.

This book is a treasure trove of art that I hope will stimulate your imagination. As you will see in the text that accompanies each painting or photograph of a garden, I focus on only one of many elements of visual language in each to help you see the relevance to your garden. For example, in Vincent van Gogh's *Road Workers in Saint Remy* (figure 5.7), I look only at the use to which he put the negative space between the trees and canvas edge, yet there are so many other elements of visual language that van Gogh employed in this painting. To further stimulate your eye, review all the paintings and garden images in this book, and perhaps in other books or museums, against these following criteria and others you devise. Then go into your garden and look at it in relation to the same elements of visual language.

The key to this whole idea rests on your willingness to really see and study these paintings, and that takes time. Research shows that most people spend three to eight seconds in front of a painting in an art museum. You can't learn much in eight seconds. Take your time. Sink into these paintings for several minutes; the rewards will astonish you. You will start seeing *everything* in a new way. Here are some ways to look at both paintings and gardens in this book and your life:

**Itinerary of the Eye:** How did the painter (or garden photographer and designer) show you the way into the image? Sometimes it's an inviting generous path, as in Joseph Pierre Birren's *Upalong* (figure 4.1), for the eye to follow, and sometimes you have to look more closely to see the subtle signals painters employ to draw your eye into and around the painting. The way in is a crucial element of good design.

**Horizontal or Vertical:** Some paintings are oriented vertically so the subject matter is "piled up" and atop one another, as in Willard Leroy Metcalf's *Dogwood Blossoms*

(No. 1) (figure 4.5). Vertical trees and then mounds of shrubs and horizontal groundcovers similarly carry the organization of some gardens. Other paintings and gardens, particularly in expansive western and midwestern landscapes, are horizontal, as in Kate Gridley's *Gordon's Pears* (figure 3.6). Look closely at every painting and garden in this book with just this one question in mind: Is the canvas oriented vertically or horizontally? What impact does that have on the painter's interpretation of subject matter? Then examine your garden for those areas that are predominantly vertical or horizontal—something you may not have created consciously. Then decide what plants and features you could add to strengthen that verti-cality or horizontality.

**The Vantage Point:** When you place a bench in your garden, you direct the view of anyone sitting on it. You establish a key vantage point. Unlike other fixed vantage points—windows and doorways in your house, for example—the placement of benches can be changed easily to emphasize different aspects of your garden. The same is true for an artist's easel; where Paul Cézanne set up his easel in *Chestnut Trees and Farmhouse of Jas de Bouffan* (figure 2.1) or where Matilda Browne set up hers in *Clarke Voorhees House* (figure 2.2) has an impact on the nature of their landscape paintings. Examine every painting and photograph in this book with vantage point in mind. Try to imagine how the painting or photograph would be different if the artist or photographer had moved to a different place in the landscape or garden. This exercise will teach you a lot about the importance of key vantage points in your garden: the top of steps; a bench or chair; the placement of a gazebo, pergola, arbor, or sitting area.

**Color:** Explore individual colors or groups of colors. For example, first look at every painting and photograph of a garden in this book only for the color red. Next look only for where painters and gardeners have juxtaposed green and blue. Then do the same in your

own house—rugs, paintings, fabrics, paint colors—and then go out to your garden. Or look at the Pierre Bonnard or Cézanne paintings in this book and notice the colors they used as opposed to those van Gogh employed. Given your interest in gardening, perhaps the most important color to look for and study in all its many shades and hues is green, for that is the color that knits a garden, and often landscape paintings, together.

**Man-Made Objects Contrasted with Natural Forms:** Start this study by going into your garden looking only for the juxtaposition of your house and the trees and shrubs planted near it. Next look only at subordinate structures like a garden shed, barn, garage, gazebo, or pergola and the natural forms of the plantings near them. Are those contrasts pleasing or jarring? Then look at all the images in this book—for example, Claude Monet's *Le Dejeuner* (figure 2.6)—to see how painters and garden designers treat this element of pleasing contrast.

**Open Sky Versus Enclosed Gardens:** Painters use the sky in different ways; so do gardeners. Examine how much sky each painter (and garden photographer) included in each canvas and photograph in this book. Then walk throughout your garden to see if you have varied your experience by showing an open view of the sky in one area yet in another you break up the view overhead with an arbor, pergola, or trees. Vary the experience overhead as well as at eye and ground levels.

**Line:** Look at each image in this book with only lines in mind. Notice how, for example, Cézanne blurs lines in favor of light in his painting *Bridge over a Pond* (figure 4.7), whereas Joseph Stella's *Old Brooklyn Bridge* (figure 4.6) is all about the interaction of related diagonal lines. Examine all other images and then your garden for not only the lines of trees and branching but also bed edges and the lines scribed by driveway and path edges to see if they relate.

**Mood:** What emotions does each painter and garden designer elicit in the images included in this book? The warmth and intimacy of a Henri Matisse interior, as in *The Bedroom* (figure 6.8), contrasts with the excitement and bravado of Emily Mason's bright sensuous colors in *Until Just Then* (figure 1.6). Paintings by van Gogh are electric with emotion, as in *Road Workers in Saint Remy* (figure. 5.7), whereas Richard Schmid's *The Russian Doll* (figure 3.4) is elegant in its restraint and subject matter. Then go into your garden and, using the list of descriptive words in Appendix C (see pages 165 and 166), attach words to the emotions you feel in various parts of your garden.

**Contrasting Forms:** Look at each image in this book with contrasting forms in mind, for this is one key element of visual language the garden designer needs to understand. Look closely at Matisse's *The Luxembourg Garden* (figure 4.3) to see how he emphasizes the juxtaposition of varying forms in hedges, shrubs, trees, and the road. Look at Camille Pissarro's *Entrée du Village de Voisins* (figure 1.2) to see how you could contrast the geometry of your house with the elongated forms of trees planted near it.

**Scale:** Take a close look at the very first painting in this book—Thomas Cole's *The Arch of Nero* (figure 1.1)—to see how Cole used the cowherd and cows in the lower right of the painting to help you understand the scale of what remains of the ancient stone fortifications. Notice how John Lee Fitch uses the fisherman in his painting *Trout Stream, Green River, Connecticut* (figure 4.2) to help you understand the size of the tree and the distance between foreground and background. In fact, thumb throughout the book to see how painters use human figures and garden designers use furniture, structures, or buildings of known size to establish scale. Then go into your garden to see what devices you have used (or could add) in your garden to help clarify scale: furniture and small buildings or structures like arbors and pergolas. After all, from a distance, we know how big a chair is, but we don't know how big a tree is.

**Visual Centers:** Paintings as well as areas within your garden need visual centers, where the visitor's visual or physical journey begins and to which all parts relate. Look at the woman on the couch in Henri Rousseau's *Le Douanier* (figure 4.9) or the balustrade at the end of the path at Stan Hywet Gardens in Akron, Ohio (figure 4.2A). Look for the visual core in each image and then go into your garden to find whether or not your individual garden areas have visual centers in the form of a garden ornament, a structure, a shorn plant, a sculpture, or a plant with striking foliage.

**Balance:** Look at each painting to see if you can discern the ways the painter has used form, color, or mass to keep a painting in balance right to left, top to bottom. Then go out to the street or sidewalk to see if you have too much visual weight to the right or left of your house. Or sit on the back terrace or on any bench in your garden to see if there's too much interest to the right or left, and how you might balance your garden from important vantage points. Balance is not necessarily symmetry. Study the ways Bonnard, for example, balances his *The Terrace at Vernon* (figure 2.5).

**Temperature:** Examine each image in the book, and each part of your garden, to take the temperature of each. You'll see what I mean. For starters, go to Mason's *Until Just Then* (figure 1.6) and then to Monet's *Summer* (figure 5.1) and you'll see the difference between hot and cool. Then go into your garden and feel the differing temperatures that come from sun or shade, color or form. Varying temperatures can heighten a visitor's, and a viewer's, experience.

**A Sense of Depth:** Matisse and Hugo Grenville are far more interested in color, form, and mass than depth. Take a look at Matisse's *Gate of the Casbah* (figure 6.6) or Hugo Grenville's *Still Life with Poppies, Orchid and Dutch Coffee Pot* (figure 6.9) and you'll see what I mean. Then look at Raoul Dufy's *The Harvest* (figure 6.4) and how he uses horses and trees in the foreground and background to establish depth. Then go into your garden to see how, or if, you have used objects or paths to establish a clear sense of the relationship between foreground and background through this method of repeating objects of known size close-up and far away.

**Passages:** There is a whole painting and then there are the parts, vignettes, passages, and details that go into making up that painting. In Bonnard's *The Terrace at Vernon* (figure 2.5), one passage is of the woman on the left looking toward her parrot with her back to you. On the other side is a second passage of a woman in a hat walking up stairs and onto the terrace. They introduce just a hint of narrative into the painting. There's also the passage of horses grazing in the far meadow, the light sparkling on the river. While the whole painting has a mood, so does each of these passages or vignettes. Look for these passages, these subplots in paintings, and in your garden. They are everywhere. Once you see them, perhaps you can add to or subtract from them to give them more clarity or impact.

"No artist ever says 'I'm going to paint a picture right now.' Many thoughts go through his or her mind before the first stroke of paint is put on a canvas, and so it is with the dedicated gardener and his or her plantings and compositions. Inspiration is the bottom line. . . . We see, absorb, winnow, and sift, and finally our imaginations take wing and out of all this come our gardening plans."

—Emily Whaley, *Mrs. Whaley and Her Charleston Garden*

"Bring your life to your work."

—ANDY GOLDSWORTHY

## STEP I
# CHOOSE YOUR STYLE

The first decision to make as you begin a garden design is what style will drive the design: formal or naturalistic, linear or curvilinear, minimalist or over the top? To help you answer this question, look at the interior and exterior of your house to gain clues as to what style will be most appropriate outside your specific house. Next, look closely at the land and come to a solid understanding of its qualities and character. Finally, follow Andy Goldsworthy's advice; look inside yourself. Ask what kind of garden you want, not what kind of garden others expect of you.

Here's another approach to answering this question: think back to what gardens or landscapes you've visited that truly moved you, and do the same with paintings. Then try to discern what the painting and landscape have in common. The search for the answer to the overall style of your garden will ride on an understanding of these three centrally important sources of inspiration—your house, your land, yourself.

To help determine that overriding style, that big idea that will inform myriad decisions, I open this book with a look at several styles—though by no means all aesthetic styles—through which both painters and garden designers express themselves. As you look at these paired images of a painting and a garden, both of similar style, pay attention to how the images make you feel. Which style appeals to you? Do you like the free flowing and curvilinear or the linear and formal? Do you like the feeling of a highly controlled garden or one that feels wild and free? Closely examining these initial pairs of images will help you clarify what your own personal style is, and it may even introduce you to styles you may not have considered.

Before getting into the substance of artistic style, let's address one key issue I came across time after time as I researched the work of specific artists. Like you, many artists have doubted themselves. But time and again, I read the words of artists who got beyond that self-doubt and simply started to paint. Richard Schmid (see figures 3.1–3.4), a nationally known landscape and portrait artist, writes this bit of advice: "Don't bother about whether or not you have talent. Just assume you do, and get to work." Paul Klee, the Austrian artist

(1879–1940), wrote, "Everyone must go where his own instinct leads him . . ." while Edouard Vuillard, the great French impressionist (1868–1940), said, "The important thing is to have faith enough [in yourself] to produce."

Or you can pay heed to no-nonsense Emily Whaley, a contemporary gardener and writer from Charleston, South Carolina, who wrote after decades of gardening: "A warning: Life is full of decisions and you better not waver and quaver over each one or you will stress yourself. You will die young and miss your seventies and eighties." Have at it.

## ROMANTICISM

As a professional garden designer working with clients nationwide, I often find myself between two spouses, one rational, the other romantic, and it's not always the woman who is romantic by any means. But here's a couple that fit the classic mold: Harold Nicholson was husband to the famous British gardener and writer Vita Sackville-West. The two of them created Sissinghurst in Kent, perhaps the most visited garden in the world. He wrote in his diary:

> In the afternoon I moon about with Vita trying to convince her that planning is an element of gardening. . . . The tragedy of the romantic temperament is that it dislikes form so much that it ignores the effect of masses. She wants to put stuff in which 'will give a lovely red in autumn.' I wish to put stuff in which will furnish shape to the perspective. In the end we part, not as friends.

In the end, it was this powerful tension and brilliant resolution between the romantic and reasoned that provides Sissinghurst with its broad and deeply felt appeal.

Romanticism as a movement in art flourished in the early nineteenth century and was a reaction to the preceding Age of Enlightenment, an age of reason: Harold followed by Vita, writ large. Romanticism in art gathered around the expression of strong emotion and dramatic effect as a source of aesthetic pleasure. Its art was bold, large scale, focused on untamed nature. The settings in romantic paintings were exotic, filled with dramatic action or scenery, often in lonely settings among evocative ruins, with one or two diminutive human figures, cows, or horses dwarfed by the grandeur of the setting.

Romantic gardens are similar. They are extravagant, enchanting, enclosed, leafy, and fragrant, appealing directly to the senses of smell, sight, and touch, uncontrolled, delightful, haphazard, alluring in their innocence, and atmospheric. Romantic gardens console in their implied harmony between man and nature.

Graham Rose, in his book *The Romantic Garden,* says that the purpose of his book is to "inspire and tell gardeners how to make (romantic) gardens that appeal to all the senses: fragrant, visually unusual and beautiful places that mute extraneous sound and which soothe the spirits; gardens that appeal to emotion rather than reason."

Stephen Lacey, in Jane Garmey's book, *The Writer in the Garden,* sums up this style:

> The romantic gardener's approach is entirely the reverse (of the classical). . . . Shapes and forms are still important considerations but they are definitely secondary ones . . . In the romantic garden (plants) are the very basis of and reason for the design. Romantic gardeners have a deep passion for plants for their own sake and the design of our gardens has to be flexible enough to cope with an ever-changing and ever increasing plant population. . . .

*Romanticism in art is gathered around the expression of strong emotion and dramatic effect as a source of aesthetic pleasure. Its art was bold, large scale, focused on untamed nature. The settings in romantic paintings were exotic, filled with dramatic action or scenery. . . . Romantic gardens are similar.*

## Romantic gardens are:
- ~ Private, secluded, tranquil places isolated from the everyday world
- ~ Serene and enclosed
- ~ Not highly maintained, so as not to show the work
- ~ Leafy and fragrant
- ~ Extravagant and enchanting
- ~ Alluring in their innocence

## Romantic gardens have:
- ~ Modern buildings at a distance or in the garden that are often screened
- ~ Views of church steeples or other idyllic views into thick woodland or broad meadows framed from within the garden
- ~ An abundance of plant life that does not appear designed
- ~ Rampant vines tumbling down from enclosing limbs overhead
- ~ Old furniture, paving materials, and sculptures evoking the passage of time

*Continued*

Figure 1.1: Thomas Cole (1801–1848), *The Arch of Nero*, 1846, in the collection of the Newark Museum, New Jersey; photographed by the museum and Art Resource, New York. A Romantic painting helps you see how to evoke a feeling of age in your new garden: old artifacts; plants laid out in an almost unkempt way, with vines falling from walls and trees.

## Painting

**An evocation of the past:** The viaduct is disintegrating; vines are growing in its decaying rubble. Cows languidly rest in a patch of sunlight in the foreground, themselves an evocation of a timeless way of life; the cowherd in white vest appears to look off into the distance toward a second decaying viaduct. Timeless hills stretch out into the distance.

**The design:** While there is an architecture to this painting—the repeated arch and viaducts anchor the work and define depth—Cole is more interested in feeling. He evokes emotions gathered around decay and a longing for a simpler past. Here is man in harmony with nature.

**Itinerary of the eye:** The color white demands attention, so painters often use it to initiate a visual journey. Your eye is drawn first to the white cow in the bottom center, then to the cowherd's white vest, and then to the grand arch framing the distant white clouds, then up to the sky and back down to the secondary arch before returning to the white cow.

**Color:** Greens, whites, and pale blues predominate and harmoniously knit the work together. This painting is not about color, not about design. It is about the harmonious evocation of mood, about longing for a lost, bucolic past, something parts or the whole of your garden might address.

Figure 1.1A: Photo by John Glover. Romanticism is embodied in the climbing hydrangea rambling up an old wall, parts of which are sloughing off. Rust on gates and errant branches on unpruned shrubs evoke the mood of letting go associated with romantic gardens.

## Garden

**An evocation of the past:** The brick wall, while certainly sound, was built to look old. Stucco has sloughed off the brick base; time has passed. The unpruned climbing hydrangea evokes the passage of time; visitors have to bend down to get through this archway and intruding vine. Mood is everything.

**The design:** This point of transition, this threshold between one garden area and a second, is about nostalgia. Too much maintenance—too refined a look—prevents this sentiment. Low levels of maintenance are central to the romantic style; plants are let go. Mark areas of transition in your garden with old gates or a rusted metal arbor up which climbing roses scramble and keep the maintenance imperfect.

**The itinerary of the eye:** The break in the wall and the finely crafted gate draw your eye to this key transition point, while at the same time the opening gives you a hint of what is to come. The visual journey in Cole's painting becomes a physical journey for you.

**Color:** No reds, blues, yellows, or bright oranges distract from this simple color palette of brick orange, white, and green. This is a quiet garden of mood, not color. As we build our gardens, we need to make conscious decisions, just as painters do, of when to introduce bright colors and when to use only muted ones.

# CLASSICAL AXIAL DESIGN

I use the term *classical* here not to evoke the art of the Romans and Greeks, nor to evoke the high period of any art form, but simply as a term that helps me get at the classic layout of a painting and a garden.

To my eye, classical gardens and paintings embody self-expression within a clear, considered, often linear form. In many ways this is the style most associated with firmly structured English gardens and as such is a style that many use across North America. This is the style comprised of straight lawn paths between perennial and shrub borders, a four-quadrant herb garden with a garden ornament on a pedestal set at the junction of its four paths, or an arbor or gazebo festooned with wisteria placed at the end of a long straight path.

Whereas Romantic gardens overflow with plants, passion, and fragrance, the classical garden, both large and small, urban and suburban, modern and historic, contains those same elements but within an often linear, axial arrangement of paths and beds. Formal or classical gardens are measured in straight hedges, fences, and paths, all of which are parallel or perpendicular to those of the house. Nothing is random.

Plants, while certainly a big part of a classical garden, are subordinate to the overall design and serve the roles of line, form, mass, and enclosure. Structure, framework, and organized spaces, often made from stone, brick, and shorn evergreens, means the formal garden is clearly designed, carefully conceived, geometric, restrained, sometimes symmetrical, and harmonious in line and form. In many ways it is the type of garden I argue for in my book *Your House, Your Garden* and the kind of garden we created in Vermont.

This type of garden is particularly appropriate near the house, where the lines of the largest structure in your garden—your house—can be answered by straight-line gardens near it. Just as the interior of the house is divided into rooms and areas, each for a particular function, so can the garden be divided up into areas and spaces, each with its own particular role in the life of your family. The object of this style of garden design is to bring house and garden into a harmonious relationship.

This is not to say a formal, classical garden cannot have a heart, as Mirabel Osler writes in a passage titled "A Gentle Plea for Chaos" in Jane Garmey's book *The Writer in the Garden:*

*The very soul of a garden is shriveled by zealous regimentation. . . . A mania for neatness, a lust for conformity and away goes atmosphere and sensuality. . . . But where is the lure? And where, alas, is seduction and gooseflesh on the arms? . . . There is a place for precision, naturally. Architectural lines such as those from hedges, paths or topiary are the bones of a garden.*

*To my eye, classical gardens and paintings embody self-expression within a clear, considered, often linear form. In many ways this is the style most associated with firmly structured English gardens and as such is a style that many use across North America.*

In the gardens I design, as well as our garden in Vermont, I try to blend clean lines with informal plantings within those lines to create a tension between control and lack thereof, between clear purpose and spontaneity. Stephen Lacey sums up classic versus Romantic garden design in his book *The Startling Jungle:*

*The very best gardens are undoubtedly those which have had the benefit of both the classical and the romantic influence, for then the pitfalls of each approach—that the classical garden tends to be too rigid and unexciting and the romantic garden tends to be wild and shapeless—are avoided.*

*Continued*

Figure 1.2: Camille Pissarro, *Entrée du Village de Voisins (Yvelines)*, 1872, in the collection of the Musée d'Orsay, Paris, France; photo by Erich Lessing/Art Resource, New York. This is "classical" only in the sense that Pissarro leads your eye down a straight path into a balanced world. Straight paths show the destination.

## Painting

**The way in:** Pissarro, on the cutting edge of impressionism in 1872, uses classic perspective to funnel your eye deep into this painting. All the radiating straight lines of the main roadway, subordinate paths, and hedges start at the base of the painting and converge on the buildings in the background. This is also a classic way to organize a garden image, with straight paths and hedges converging on a single object.

**Destination for the eye:** Pissarro draws your eye to the two dray horses by having the lines of the roadway converge on that spot. The blocky building directly above the horses is the center of the painting; its hard white edge contrasts sharply with the dark shadows in the trees behind it. Painter Richard Schmid told me that when he wants to draw attention to a particular point in a painting he puts his lightest light against the darkest dark. A white bench against a yew hedge would do the same.

**Unity and coherence:** Strong diagonals of the roadway and paths in the foreground provide framework; Pissarro throws secondary diagonals in the shadow lines of trees to the left across the diagonals of the roadway to further unify the painting. Two sets of trees to the right and left frame the central image vertically and hold your eye in a coherent space. The benign blue sky overhead unifies.

**Defining depth and scale:** Pissarro places a person in the lower-left corner to establish scale. We can also compare the size of that person with the second gray-clothed person standing by the horse deeper into the painting to understand distance. You could use a bench, an object of known size, in your garden to clarify scale and establish a clear sense of depth.

Figure I.2A: The Long Borders in the author's garden photographed by Richard Brown. The straight lawn path between two mixed shrubs and perennial borders with a clear destination at the end of the path is a classic way to organize a garden; there are no mysteries.

## Garden

**The way in:** I begin every design with paths. They provide primary framework, just as Pissarro used the roadway in his painting. I next turn to built structures such as a gazebo, with its promise of shelter and respite, to draw people down paths and towards a destination. When paths, built structures, and adjacent beds relate harmoniously in this way, a classic and comfortable garden results.

**Destination for the eye:** A garden, like a painting, needs a central focus, a place on which your eye first comfortably alights. Once satisfied, your eye then sets off on an exploration of what is around that central object, frequently returning to a reassuring center. The gazebo and finely crafted furniture provide that focus.

**Unity and coherence:** The geometric relationship between the straight lawn path and geometric gazebo provides unity through mathematical relationships. It's the lines on which details hang. Within the beds, coherence is formed by repeated elements. One example is the repetition of the burgundy red-leaved barberries (now replaced by *Physocarpus opulifolius* 'Diablo') every twenty feet or so up the center of the ten-foot-wide beds. At eye level, we repeated important ornamental grasses and other large-scale herbaceous perennials irregularly down the length of both beds.

**Defining depth:** Everyone knows the size of a bench, so visitors to our garden can subliminally understand distance in relation to that bench under the gazebo.

# IMPRESSIONISM

The impressionists were the first to explore the idea that light itself, rather than the object lit, is the subject of art. In doing so, they show us how to see in a new way. Go into your garden, squint your eyes, and you'll see what they meant. It is not the individual plants and flowers that are of interest to these painters but the play of light on those plants, on the surface of water, on the leaves of trees. The impressionists are central to modern gardening. They ushered in whole new ways of seeing nature and, therefore, began a redefinition of what a garden is. It is in this new view, gathered around light itself, that we as gardeners today can learn so very much.

Before the impressionists' first exhibit in Paris in 1874, nature was simply not the subject of art except when it was used in grand monumental paintings of towering mountains and crashing seas, or it was the backdrop for monumental theatrical subjects. The impressionists were the first to see that the effect of light on objects could be *the* subject of art. Their paintings are so popular, in part, because they strike chords of optimism, vibrancy, and color; for example, the play of light and shadow on a field of poppies or the shimmer of water reflecting the sky punctuated by blooming water lilies. But rarely do you see recognizable plants in impressionist paintings. The perfect representational paintings of the pre-Raphaelites working in England at the same time was not of much interest to the French who saw color—shimmering, delicate, vibrating color—as their true subject.

The impressionists teach us how to see beauty—extraordinary beauty—in the everyday, and it is a lesson that is so very rich and varied and stimulating that you will never see the world the same way again if you come to truly see in the same way impressionist painters saw.

Impressionism started in France in the 1860s and developed as a reaction against the Salon. This conservative body of jurists with their annual exhibits determined the nature and content of art up until the first impressionist show in Paris in 1874. The academic approach to art was formulaic. The subjects were limited to historical, religious, or classical themes, and the presentation of these subjects was theatrical and monumental. Academic painters focused on action or a group of figures placed in the center of the canvas. They painted their subjects using deep rich colors and applied paint so as to create a perfectly finished surface that showed no trace of brush on canvas. Nature was in the background. Even after the impressionists gained notoriety, the equivalent in gardening was the bedding-out approach of the Victorians where proscribed massed pelargoniums, for example, were laid out within the Jardin des Tuileries in Paris or in the municipal bedding of begonias in England and America to form vast monochromatic arrays of color.

The radical impressionists reacted against the straitjacket of the French Academy and ushered in a series of changes that transformed art, just as William Robinson and Gertrude Jekyll began their revolution against the stultifying and proscribed English gardening approaches of the late 1800s. The impressionists chose to paint everyday scenes that captured the fleeting moment of people boating, having lunch in a woodland, a woman and child walking in a field of poppies, seascapes, or ducks paddling in a pool. Nature, in their eyes, was a subject worthy of their attention. They painted what they saw, and did not idealize it: the streets of Paris, the world of ballet, haystacks, the faces of cathedrals, and their own gardens or those of others. But, in fact, their new subject was light.

They saw that color is light reflecting off objects. They were endlessly interested in light, atmosphere, weather, and outdoor subjects, where natural light would become the center of their attention. Their work was characterized by vibrant, light, bright, and airy paintings that placed color over line as their organizing force. They started cropping images in new ways and relaxed the boundary between foreground and background. They painted in broad brushstrokes and mixed paint right on the canvas in such a way that their brushstrokes were in many ways a record of their process. They took painting out of the studio and into the fields, forests, cities, towns, and public parks of France to begin painting *en plein air,* an approach in part made possible by the invention in the mid-1840s of the collapsible and sealable tin paint tube along with manufactured paints of consistent color that could be stored and kept fresh in those tubes.

As Derek Fell points out in his book *The Impressionist Garden,* impressionism was developing in tandem with two other social changes: a middle class was emerging from the successes of the Industrial Revolution and horticulture was becoming one of its primary interests. Many impressionist painters also had gardens that became the subject for many of their paintings: Claude Monet's garden at Giverny—the subject of over five hundred of his paintings—is clearly the most famous, but there were others: Édouard Manet, Mary Cassatt, Gustave Caillebotte, and Frederic Bazille all had gardens, while Berthe Morisot, Pierre-Auguste Renoir, and Alfred Sisley visited and painted gardens. Impressionists used plants in a very new way that we take for granted today. They used flower color as they used paint, to create color combinations: striking contrasts like blue irises and orange calendulas or gentle juxtapositions of pink roses underplanted with pink carnations and pink peonies and gray-leaved santolina. Their paintings can still show us how to see color, how to juxtapose color, how to create shimmering and evanescent gardens, even within linear bed arrangements similar to those of formal gardens. But if there is any one lesson we can learn from viewing impressionist art, it is to pay attention to light and how it determines color.

Marcel Proust, the great French writer, summed up impressionism this way:

*If, one day, I can see Claude Monet's garden, I feel certain that what I shall see there is a garden of tones and colors more than of flowers, is a garden less the old florist garden than a colorist garden, if I may call it that, of flowers arranged in a whole that is not entirely that of nature, since they have been planted in such a way that only those flowers blossom together whose shades match, harmonize infinitely in a blue or pink expanse, and which this powerfully revealed intention on the part of the painter has dematerialized, in a way, from all that is not color.*

*Continued*

Figure I.3: Childe Hassam (1859–1935), *In the Garden (Celia Thaxter in her Garden)*, 1892, in the collection of and photographed by the Smithsonian American Art Museum, Washington, D.C., and Art Resource, New York. The sunny impressionist garden is about the play of light on flowers and objects; here, Thaxter and her garden are one, bathed in the same sparkling light.

## Painting

**Structure:** The base of the painting is a play of soft greens interspersed with its complement, red. A subtle gap in those greens arcs toward the focus of the painting, Celia Thaxter herself. Tall hollyhocks to right and left frame her. Hassam releases the very top of the painting into the atmosphere. (You can decide when to release areas of your garden to the sky, and when to hold the garden close to the ground with the branches of trees overhead.) In the middle left stands Thaxter next to a contrasting stone fence post that anchors her and, with its pair, frames a view out to sea.

**The play of light:** The clarity of light on the Isle of Shoals, many miles off the coast of Maine, must have been sparkling clear when Hassam painted Thaxter in her garden over a hundred years ago. Certainly we know from the painting that Thaxter grew hollyhocks

and poppies, but what she really loved was color suffused by light.

**Color harmony:** Soft pastels harmonize everything: garden, sea, sky, and the gentle presence of Thaxter herself. She is not delineated any more clearly than her garden; the two are one. Choosing color schemes for seaside gardens is eased by choosing those that will complement the soft blues, pinks, grays, and lavenders of the sea and sky.

**Overlap and unity:** Color harmony unifies the painting, as does the overlapping of subjects. Flower stems overlap Thaxter's dress, linking her to the garden. She overlaps the horizon line and the sky, linking all three. The fence post near her overlaps sea and just a bit of sky; hollyhocks overlap sea and sky.

Figure I.3A: The spring garden in the author's garden. In mid-April, sunlight filters through clouds of tiny white flowers on our wild plums to highlight the yellows, pinks, and whites in the flowers below.

## Garden

**Structure:** Gardens go through impressionist stages. In mid-April every year, the wild plums bloom in our spring garden, throwing a canopy over daffodils, primulas, and a pink *Rhododendron mucronulatum*. The white canopy overhead is answered on the ground by dark greens as well as yellows and whites; the diagonal gray stepping-stone path carries your eye and body into the space, while the English staddle stone anchors the beginning of that path and contrasts, like the granite fence posts in Hassam's painting, with the natural forms of plants. The stark angular trunks and branches of the wild plums provide a wild vertical structure; every two trunks or branches frame space between them.

**The play of light:** Sunlight coming down through the transparent white blooms suffuses this garden with a clear light that makes the white and yellow blooms at ground level glow. That light illuminates all the textures of emerging European ginger, daylilies, aquilegias, ferns, and epimediums, as well as the yellow-flowering wild oats in the background. Red tulips provide punches of color. Notice how Hassam used those same punches of red.

**Color harmony:** The primary harmony of greens, whites, and yellows is accented by pink and red in the background. The gray stepping-stones contrast with the color harmony to show the way in.

**Overlap and unity:** The black trunks of the trees provide verticality and visually link the ground to the lawn, hedges, distant misty meadows, and trees, as well as the sky because their trunks overlap everything in the near and distant view.

# CUBISM

*Cubists used abstract fragmented shapes to depict several views of the same object simultaneously. Their paintings were collages of interlocking shapes and volumes as seen from varying perspectives.*

James Rose, one of the first graduates of Harvard's new landscape architecture program in the early 1930s, was a proponent of cubism and its interlocking shapes as inspiration for garden design just over a decade after cubism had run its course. On two occasions in 1991, I visited James Rose at his home in Ridgewood, New Jersey. He told me that he had studied at the Landscape Design School at Harvard in the early 1930s with classmates Dan Kiley and Garret Eckbo, both of whom went on to influential careers that redefined landscape architecture and garden design in America. Kiley, who worked from his offices in Vermont, created linear, spare, classic designs. Rose took a very different path inspired by cubism, a style he held true to throughout his fifty-year career.

Pablo Picasso (1881–1973) and Georges Braque (1882–1963) were the two artists who developed cubism, an art movement that ran from roughly 1907 to 1914. They used abstract fragmented shapes to depict several views of the same object simultaneously. Their paintings were collages of interlocking shapes and volumes as seen from varying perspectives simultaneously. Both artists acknowledge that Paul Cézanne's earlier experiments with multiple perspectives—a tabletop seen from above with a teapot on it seen from below and a bowl of oranges sitting impossibly on the tilted table seen from a forty-five-degree angle—paved the way for cubism.

Both Picasso and Braque painted a woman playing a guitar, for example, from many angles simultaneously, thereby rendering the female figure in the form of interpenetrating shapes. As cubists, Braque and Picasso developed little or no sense of depth in their painting. Furthermore, they used a narrow range of muted colors—browns, beiges, blacks, and grays—so as to emphasize the integration of forms, just as Rose emphasized only greens in plants and grays in materials. The cubist painters broke recognizable forms into a number of integrated facets, such as a bowl of fruit or a table with candlesticks and playing cards atop it. In doing so, they broke with the impressionists who were painting recognizable objects in space that had depth.

During the days I interviewed Rose, he spoke frequently about cubism and its role in his work. He also spoke at length about the many visits he had made to the gardens of Japan. The link between these two disciplines—cubism in art and the eastern approach to garden design—became very clear to me as Rose talked and as he showed me not only his own garden but also those of his clients.

In 1967, Reinhold Publishing in New York published his *Modern American Gardens—Designed by James Rose*. The text was written by Marc Snow, a pseudonym. Rose wrote in the early part of the book: "European garden design up to the year 1937 had evolved toward a modern style while retaining classical principles. The influence of the contemporary movements—Futurism, Cubism, Surrealism, and Modern architecture—effected landscape design." Always the creative renegade, Rose looked for a new style and new way to develop both residential and commercial sites; he turned to cubism for inspiration.

I learned what he meant when he showed me the Werlin Garden in Englewood, New Jersey. Two of his installers were building a boxy landscape planter comprised of four right angles. That is, the men were building a rectangular shape in a garden that was otherwise comprised of oblique angles in walls, bed edges, and paths. Rose explained to the men that no pure geometric shape could be allowed in the garden as it would "lift" right out of the overall design. Geometric shapes would not integrate with the other more oblique shapes but would remain separate from the lines of paths, planting beds, the swimming pool, and furniture placement. As Rose walked me through eleven gardens he designed, I saw not one right angle, circle, or arc on a radius. All shapes were comprised of interrelated oblique angles, thereby creating a totally integrated cubist work.

Here is a caption for a photograph in Rose's book, a caption that could just as well be describing a cubist painting: "A succession of spaces flows from one to the other—planes intersect, the materials and forms are more a guidance than an interruption. As one wanders through these spaces, the forms become part of the space and the viewer part of both. The experience is seen as changing from form to space, to landscape to object to place. . . ."

To ensure the unity of these interrelated shapes and form, Rose used virtually no flowering perennials in his designs—notwithstanding the Siberian iris and the daylily—for fear yellows, blues, reds, and violets, even chartreuse would break the otherwise green uniformity of his designs. He did not want colorful perennials to leap out of the overall design and demand undue attention. He worked with greens, especially evergreens such as hemlocks, pines, and rhododendrons,

as well as green-leaved birches and, now and again, dogwoods, honeylocusts, and cutleaf maples.

It was largely materials that drove the cubism of his gardens: asymmetric wooden decks and steps, stone-paved terraces, boulders, river rocks, and water in obliquely angled pools. His interest was in creating what the cubists had created: the interpenetration of forms. Surfaces intersect at seemingly random angles presenting no coherent sense of depth or traditional design. He used only irregular bluestone straight from the quarry; I never saw a piece of cut stone in his designs.

Yet what he did, and you could do if this style appeals to you, was to create an overall pattern for house and garden that would not have a beginning, middle, or end. It would have edges, where house meets garden, for example, but Rose would blur those edges, as he did in his own house, with big sheets of glass and sliding glass doors. As we sat in one room, I saw how the material inside a floor-to-ceiling window was the same outside that window. The house reached into the garden in the form of a bedroom and then the garden would reach into the house as a wall of the dining room receded to make room for a planted space. House and garden were integrated; forms of architecture penetrated the garden and vice versa.

Let me put this another way. I went to visit Rose to talk about my idea for a book on the garden path and its role in starting good garden design. He balked at this notion and said, "Tell me where the path ends and the garden begins. If you've designed an integrated coherent space, it is all garden—path and plants and beds and water. There are no edges, no differentiation, only integration."

*Continued*

Figure 1.4: Georges Braque (1882–1963), *Road Near L'Estaque*, 1908, in the collection of the Museum of Modern Art, New York City; licensed by SCALA/Art Resource, New York; © 2008 Artists Rights Society, New York/ADAGP, Paris, France. Plates of color organized by forceful diagonals on the ground contrast with the freer forms of tree foliage; cut stone or wooden walkways can help you achieve this look in your garden.

## Painting

**Itinerary of the eye.** Like so much traditional art, Braque, in this early cubist piece, continues to show us a clear way into the image. This road near L'Estaque has been cut into a hillside; a retaining wall holds the road level, and our eye follows that road deep into the center of the picture.

**Keeping your eye in:** Braque uses classic techniques to keep your eye in the canvas, just as you need to do in your garden. The branches of the tree on the left stop your eye from wandering off the canvas; the arcing tree trunk with a white flash of sunlight on it holds your eye; the arc of that tree trunk is echoed in two other trees further up the road. The far left tree trunk sweeps to the upper left corner of the painting; Braque then carries that same sweep in a blue-green arc that ends in a yellow budlike shape that draws your eye to the white tip of the tree trunk and back down to the lower right.

**Focus on the path:** Plates of color slide down the hillside to become the surface of the road, thereby visually linking hillside to road. The flow of the road from lower right into the very center of the painting provides the focus for this work.

**A limited color palette unifies:** Braque limits himself to greens, yellows, and blues, the colors of earth and sky in the south of France. The result is coherence, one you could easily employ in your garden.

**Line and color provide movement:** The strong outlines of the plates of color as well as the outline of the retaining wall provide movement within the plates of color. The juxtaposition of these highly contrasting colors generates visual movement.

Figure I.4A: A garden by James Rose, photographed by the author. Like Braque, Rose simplifies his garden design: wooden walkways form strong plates and diagonals that contrast with a limited number of greens.

## Garden

**Itinerary—the path:** The focus is as much on the path as it is on the plants. In fact, the flow and action of lines created by the path lies in direct contrast to the mounded evergreens. The path, steps, and landings carry the cubist roots of this design.

**Keeping your eye in:** Rose created private enclosed spaces. He designed self-contained places that felt distant from roads, towns, and houses.

**Focus on the path:** The focus of his gardens was often on the paths and how they morphed into living spaces. He created many broad wooden decks surrounded with evergreen plants. It was the relationship of one flat shape to mounded evergreens that drew his attention. Imagine looking down at this image from above, and you'll see how it is cubist in its interlocking but nongeometric shapes.

**A limited plant/color palette unifies:** Rose limited his plant list largely to evergreen shrubs and groundcovers—hemlocks, pines, rhododendrons, pachysandra—as well as nonflowering trees such as honeylocusts, oaks, and maples so as not to have any one flowering plant draw attention away from the whole. While the rhododendrons certainly bloomed, it was for a brief period; Rose could not have been less interested.

**Line provides movement:** The lines formed by wooden landscape-tie walls provide the visual movement in this garden. Lines shoot out at many angles and at different levels to animate the garden while framing irregular bluestone steps.

# MINIMALISM

Minimalism is a twentieth-century art movement succinctly explained by Frank Stella (1936– ), one of its artists: "What you see is what you see." Minimalists want to reduce art to its barest bones, its absolute essence. They used, and continue to use, the absolute minimum of colors, shapes, lines, and textures to create their paintings and architecture. There is no attempt to represent or symbolize anything. Piet Mondrian, an abstract painter and precursor of the modern minimalist school, clearly influenced a number of modern minimalist garden designers, including landscape architect Anthony Paul, who lives in England and designs gardens throughout Europe and in his native land of New Zealand.

This school of minimalist abstract painting as practiced by Mondrian and minimalist painting as practiced by such contemporary artists as Robert Mangold, Ellsworth Kelly, and Frank Stella, among many others, carried over into minimalist garden design characterized by attributes such as purity, simplicity, clean lines, geometric shapes, no ornamentation, and by sleek and masterfully constructed surfaces, and by being tranquil, pared down, and of the mind.

Minimalism suggests utter restraint—Mies van der Rohe's "Less is more." It is a form of art in tune with technology and a means of disciplined expression. Minimalist garden design emphasizes materials over plants: stone, gravel, glass, wood, reinforced concrete, masonry, steel, plastic, and stucco form backdrops and contexts for single-specimen plants displayed against stark, built backdrops. Often, minimalist designs are enclosed with high walls. There is a clarity of expression about their art and gardens, a coolness, some would even say coldness, that is understated yet dramatic in its simplicity and high, engineered, cerebral design that can feel stark in its modernity. Minimalist garden designers use plants architecturally and sparingly, silhouetting individual plants with clean outlines against monochrome walls so the plants become sculptural, geometric architectural shapes.

At the same time, minimalist gardens harken back to some of the contemplative Chinese and Japanese garden design principles embodied in such gardens as the fifteenth-century garden of contemplation at Ryoan-ji Temple in Kyoto. There, Japanese garden designers used color in broad monochromatic panels, similar to the work of the Mexican architect Luis Barragan, who designed minimalist gardens around many of his buildings. In the words of Christopher Bradley-Hole, a minimalist garden designer, Barragan emphasized "pure interconnecting spaces defined by a framework of brightly coloured walls, punctuated by light and water." Minimalism does not cover walls with plants, but as Christopher Bradley-Hole writes, the minimalist garden designer:

*. . . celebrates the boundaries by keeping them uncluttered and unplanted. . . . Plain walls of pleasing proportions become features in their own right and thus key elements in the successful execution of a design. Common to all these gardens is a celebration of enclosed space and an undeniable sense of unity. The minimalist garden uses few components, thereby allowing the spectator to enjoy the spaces between the elements. . . . With the minimalist approach, plants are . . . displayed as if they were an object in an art gallery.*

*Minimalists want to reduce art to its barest bones, its absolute essence. They used, and continue to use, the absolute minimum of colors, shapes, lines, and textures to create their paintings and architecture.*

Minimalist gardens are:
- ~ Uncluttered
- ~ Pure
- ~ Simple
- ~ Tranquil
- ~ Pared down
- ~ Sculptural
- ~ Understated yet dramatic

Minimalist gardens have:
- ~ An absolute minimum of colors
- ~ Few varying textures
- ~ Clean lines
- ~ Geometric architectural shapes
- ~ No ornamentation
- ~ Sleek surfaces

*Continued*

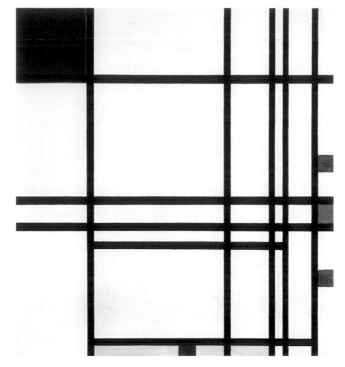

Piet Mondrian (1872–1944), *Composition No. 8*, 1939–42, with Red, Blue and Yellow; © 2008 Mondrian/Holtzman Trust. Mondrian used the painting to create harmony and balance. The black lines of the grids were always painted first; the color added later.

## Painting

**A paring down to the essentials:** During his early years, Mondrian was a traditional landscape painter. In his early thirties, he began to veer toward abstraction as a result of his growing studies in theosophy and its search for simplification. In his deep dislike of the untidiness of nature, he veered away from representational art and toward what he saw as the essence of nature: line, geometric shapes, and the primary colors on white.

**Color:** Mondrian utterly simplifies color relationships by focusing on the three primary colors displayed on a white backdrop. He further limits the interplay of color by separating those three colors from one another with thick black borders. I have seen gardens in England that mimic this approach: 4 x 4-foot planting beds, each planted with a different flowering perennial, all beds surrounded by gray peastone paths.

**Line:** Black lines separate blocks of color and divide the white backdrop into squares and rectangles. This minimalist grid approach became his style after 1919 and was, as he wrote, his attempt to "reach the foundation of things."

**Visual weight and balance:** This is a vertical painting with much of the visual weight in the bottom half of the painting. This base is comprised of blocks of blue, red, yellow, and black along the bottom and side of the lower half of the paintin. In the top half of the painting, Mondrian reduces the visual weight by including only one red panel. Furthermore, he puts no black band atop the uppermost white rectangle, thereby releasing the visual weight into the atmosphere. I am struck by echoes in the composition of this painting and Childe Hassam's *In the Garden* (figure 1.3): a weighty base, the horizon line, and the release at the top.

Figure 1.5A: Garden design by Anthony Paul. Like Mondrian, Paul asks, "What is an entry garden?" His answer: stone to walk on, green shrubs on a grid, a tree. Like Mondrian, he pares back to the utterly essential.

## Garden

**A paring down to essentials:** In this garden in Surrey, England, Paul strips the entry garden to its essence: green, clipped, low boxwoods. He took the idea of the English pattern garden and turned it on its head.

**Color:** Most entry gardens in the English tradition are comprised of stone or brick paths with profusely flowering shrubs and perennials through which paths lead. That tradition calls for color, for blousy blues and pinks, reds, and yellows. Paul strips that idea to its bones. Like Mondrian, he is reaching "for the foundation of things."

**Line:** First, Paul creates pattern not only with the lines of boxwood that comprise the shapes but he also creates lines by leaving gaps between those shapes. Second, the alignment of the boxwood shapes as well as the paths between them all relate to the strong geometry of the house. Linearity, and the geometric outlining of shapes, is central to this design, just as with Mondrian. I might add that the element of surprise as one arrives at this classic English country home is surely not lost on Paul, who revels in the unexpected.

**Visual weight and balance:** This pattern, repeated on the other side of the path to the front door, has to come out and away from the house as far as it does to be in scale with and balance the visual weight of the house. Had Paul made the garden shallower, its role would have been diminished.

# ABSTRACT EXPRESSIONISM

Abstract expressionism was initially a wholly American post–World War II art movement. Its major painters—Willem de Kooning, Hans Hoffman, Mark Rothko, Jackson Pollock, and Helen Frankenthaler, among many others—produced spontaneous abstract paintings that welled up from the subconscious rather than from rational decisions. The creation of a totally integrated form, often comprised of large interrelated free-form shapes of different colors, was one of their precepts. The whole canvas is treated with equal importance to create an overall effect, unlike classical painting where the center of focus might draw more attention while the edges would draw less. Abstract expressionists apply paint on large canvases rapidly to show raw, pure emotion. Their art was and is abstract, nonrepresentational, and nongeometric. It has the appearance of chance and accident; it appears spontaneous and utterly expressive, yet underneath, there is clearly a degree of control and purpose gathered around balance, color theory, and overall unity, though the surface of the painting is meant to appear as anything but controlled. This is an art that seeks to convey emotion through integrated color, shape, and space.

Abstract expressionism as practiced by Emily Mason, the wife of painter Wolf Kahn and the second of three generations of women abstract painters, is embodied in the following quotations from an interview I had with her:

~ "This style is based on self-discovery. I don't worry about the end result; I have faith in my own intuition. And that faith is based on self-confidence. Go for energy in the painting and the garden."

~ "My process is to discover what the painting will become. I heard John Cage, the modern composer, speak years ago, and he said before the performance of his work, 'I want to get my mind out of the way.' That's me too."

~ "There is no guarantee when you start. You put intuition on the line and when your intuition leads to a successful painting, it is *so* rewarding."

~ "Each painting is an exploration of color and color is psychologically revealing."

~ "Color and form are one."

~ "I go to a blank canvas with a blank mind. I want to play with colors. I want to get a conversation going between and among the colors on the canvas. That is, I'll put one color down and then a second, and the second affects the first. I'll put an orange down, for example, next to a purple, and it will be too hot, so I'll cool it down. I look to see what the paint will do, how it will affect me and how it will change."

~ "I want to avoid the static. I sometimes will be developing a painting and get stuck, so I'll turn it on its side or upside down just to get me unstuck. That's how you learn, by exploring, by staying unstuck."

It's easy to see how Mason would approach the development of her own garden in Vermont. Just replace the word *painting* in all her quotes above with the word *garden*. When I asked Mason to tell me about her garden, she said, "It's a set of enthusiasms. I don't plan, I explore. And I explore especially with color. For example, one time I combined daylilies in oranges, reds, and yellows with poppies and then placed blue irises in their midst." Mason might be the very model you have been looking for. Explore. Get unstuck.

## Emily Mason (1932– )

Mason, her mother Alice Trumbull Mason (1904–1971), and her daughter Emily Mason embody three generations of American abstract painters, all based in New York City. She studied art at Bennington College in Vermont and subsequently at Cooper Union in New York City. She married artist Wolf Kahn in 1957. As a young artist in New York City in the 1950s, she met and was influenced by many of the great artists of the day: Ilya Bolotowsky, Piet Mondrian, Jackson Pollock, and Willem de Kooning, to name a few. She began teaching painting at Hunter College in New York City in 1979 and continues to do so. She lives with her husband in New York City and has a home in Vermont, where she has gardens that she calls her "collection of enthusiasms," and in which she explores color combinations. In her New York studio and apartment, she surrounds herself with plants; she looks through a scrim of potted plants at every window out into the city.

*Continued*

Figure 1.6: Emily Mason, a contemporary artist, *Until Just Then*, 1999; © 2008 Emily Mason/licensed by VAGA, New York. Mason gives you permission to let go, to explore, to express yourself, to allow colors to collide and shapes and forms to break out of the boxes we often retreat into when we doubt ourselves.

## Painting

**The way in on stepping-stones:** The artist told me, "I am not at all interested in the itinerary of the eye." In this writer's humble opinion, however, I think there is one in this painting. It starts in the lower-left corner with the dripping orange stroke. Your eye starts there and travels to the cooling green patch atop its complement, a red patch, and then follows an arc on five stepping-stones toward the upper-right corner. The white band then leads across the painting, where it delivers you to the right side and then the full length of that blue stroke, the path's destination.

**Corners and edges anchored to keep your eye in:** Mason marks the lower-right corner of her painting with a light and a dark green stroke, the upper right by a blue circular stroke atop red, the upper left by blue strokes atop red. The bottom needs no anchor as the arc of stepping-stones holds your attention; on the right side, the terra-cotta patch with green and blue holds

your eye while the white band holds the top and the vermillion patch on the left holds that. Your eye whirls within a space controlled by the artist's intuitive design.

**The focal point, the heart of the matter:** Mason told me she thought she was finished with this painting, but as she stood back, she felt something was missing. She reached down for the brush in the blue paint and in one stroke added the blue check. It wasn't *until just then* that she felt the painting was complete.

**Color contrasts:** Complementary colors blue and orange and red and green are suffused with the heat of yellow and a quiet nod to lavender blue. "I am very aware of temperature in my paintings," says Mason. "There is a lot of heat in my work, but I can have too much, so I sometimes have to cool it off, in this case with some green. A painting, or garden, can't be unrelenting."

Figure I.6A: John Beedle's photograph of heleniums, eryngiums, daylilies, and ornamental grasses against a purple backdrop. Gardens are by their very nature controlled, but the abstract expressionists show us the way to be more expressive with color and texture combinations and hands-off maintenance.

## Garden

**Temperature:** The expressive designer of this garden is not afraid to turn up the heat. Hot reds, yellows, and pinks predominate, cooled only by green foliage, the blue-gray eryngiums in the center, and the violet wall at the back. As with Mason's painting, that stroke of blue in the center is crucial to the success of this garden.

**An expressive style:** The uncontrolled intermingling of plants, especially the grasses, keeps the garden from becoming tidy Edwardian blocks of distinct color.

Even Beedle, the photographer, got caught up in this and allowed the red flowers in the foreground to remain out of focus.

**Green as unifier:** Green foliage of many shapes knits this garden image together. Strap-shaped leaves of daylilies and the filmy foliage of grasses combine with the broad tree leaves to provide a wild green matrix.

# PATTERN AND DECORATION

The school of pattern and decoration was an American art movement during the 1970s and 1980s formed as a reaction against the cool minimalist, abstract, and nonrepresentational art in vogue at the time. The artists who worked within this approach—and who were often derided by the more high-minded abstract artists of the day—turned toward such decorative sources as Japanese kimonos, Mayan weavings, Islamic architectural decoration, Mexican tiles, Moroccan ceramics, and Persian manuscripts, as well as garden images to create complex, ornamented, lyrical paintings. Their works were fresh, new, simply beautiful, and often formed on a grid that gave their work an underlying elegant structure and a one-dimensional appearance. Their art was often presented in exacting large-scale paintings, appearing hedonistic, opulent, sensuous, and accessible compared to the cerebral minimalist art of the day. It was an art rich in color and texture, affirmative, complex, ornamented, and warm.

Whereas cubism gives you inspiration for the layout of your garden and encourages you to choose from a very limited plant palette, whereas abstract expressionism can encourage you to follow your impulses as you design a layout and highly personal plant combinations, pattern and decoration not only provides you with another broad idea for layout—big perennial and annual beds with color, color, color, and pattern—but also provides you with quite specific ideas for plant selection and juxtaposition.

Roger Sandes, a Vermont-based painter from the pattern and decoration school, in a painting titled *Country Life with Cows,* juxtaposes orange and yellow sunflowers with purple monkshood (*Aconitum napellus*) and the annual pink cosmos. He pointed out to me that the strong purples, oranges, and yellows make the light pink even more delicate. Another contrast—this among the leaves of these same plants—also becomes an element you can emulate: the chartreuse leaves of cosmos, the dark green foliage of sunflowers, the deeply incised deep green leaves of monkshood. Of course, as a gardener and painter, you see these colors against the background of the many blues of the sky, which, again being a complement of orange, makes those sunflowers even more vibrant. Sandes told me of other plant combinations he has used in his garden: peachy-apricot daylilies next to deep purple-black ones; pink lilies with red or terra-cotta heleniums; pale white daylilies with a yellow tint next to mauve bee balm. He also juxtaposes intense flowers in the primary colors next to their pastels.

As Sandes also pointed out, to make a good flower painting, and a good perennial garden, you need lots of greens to tie the parts together in a vital interesting way: bright chartreuse and yellow green, forest green, silver green, blue green, olive green. You also need to vary the texture and shape of the leaves that carry all those greens. It helps to know that foliage can be broken down into basically three forms: bold broad leaves like that of a ligularia or a lady's mantle, swordlike leaves as in daylilies or Siberian irises, and lacey leaves such as those of astilbes and coreopsis. By combining varying green leaves of contrasting textures with flowers that contrast, you create a visually stimulating painting and garden.

Color, pattern, and decoration are three elements many gardeners want to include in their gardens. Each adds personality, warmth, and vitality. More than any other model offered in this chapter, this American art movement provides you with the visual principles that help you create plant combinations based on pleasing contrasts in color and texture.

*The school of pattern and decoration found inspiration in Japanese kimonos, Mayan weavings, Islamic architectural decoration, Mexican tiles, Moroccan ceramics, and Persian manuscripts.*

## Roger Sandes (1941–)

He was born in Milwaukee, Wisconsin, and grew up in the small town of Wauwatosa. His father was a businessman, and his mother a homemaker. Sandes said, "No one lifted a finger to encourage my interest in art except my aunt." Three or even four times a year, Sandes and his brother visited their aunt in Chicago, Illinois, and she invariably took them to the Art Institute there. He studied art in high school, studied comparative literature for three years at the University of Wisconsin in Milwaukee, and took a few courses in the evening at the Layton School of Art in Milwaukee. In 1965, he moved to New York City to study acting at the Neighborhood Playhouse School of the Theater, where he met, on the first day, his wife to be, Mary Welsh. They lived in the city for ten years but on several occasions had extended visits to Italy, Spain, the South of France, and England. During these ten years, Sandes developed his skills as a self-taught artist, first with pen and ink, later with acrylics. (Mary started her work as a collage artist while they were living in the South of France, an art she continues to pursue.) Their son Sam was born in New York. In 1975, they moved to Wisconsin; their son Rupert was born there. Roger and Mary continued to create their work but given that many of the galleries showing their work were in the east, they moved to southern Vermont, where they have lived since 1978. They now have extensive flower gardens from which Roger paints. He has exhibited and held one-man shows across America as well as in Mexico and London, and his bright optimistic work hangs in many corporate headquarters throughout America. (Go to rockriverartists.com for more information.)

Figure 1.7: Roger Sandes, contemporary artist, *Local Events*, 2003, by permission of the artist; photograph by Jeff Baird. Combining plants that contrast pleasingly is at the heart of good garden design. Study how this artist gently contrasts each plant with its neighbors through contrasting color, form, and texture.

## Painting

**Structure:** The surround of this 38 x 49-inch painting is like three slightly different hedges around a perennial garden. These three bands of color frame a view of white oriental lilies with terra-cotta spots, blue delphiniums with black bees, pink coneflowers, and the annual brown-eyed calliopsis (*Coreopsis tinctoria*) running up through the three perennials. The diagonal lean of the flower stems adds movement.

**Foliage color combination:** The foundation of the painting within the three frames is a variation on the color green: the deep green foliage of the lilies, the brighter echinacea leaves, the olive chartreuse of the calliopsis, and the lighter green of the delphiniums. Squint your eyes and you'll see the greens hold all other colors within a unifying yet varied matrix.

**Flower color combination:** Sandes combined soft pastel pinks, yellows, and blues contrasted with sparks of black dots. The pastels, including the even softer blue sky and white clouds, set off the little black and brown dots and vise versa. These soft colors in the interior panel contrast also with the three border panels, which feature gold and iron oxide.

Figure I.7A: Andrew Lawson's photograph of a Tom Stuart-Smith design for a garden at Broughton Grange, United Kingdom. Like Sandes, the designer uses dark rills and the pool to frame plants he juxtaposed so each shows off the qualities of its neighbors. Repeated yews provide an inner loose structure.

## Garden

**Structure:** Just as Sandes framed his painting, so did Stuart-Smith frame his garden. The long narrow rill and the rectangular pool at the far end of the garden contain and thereby intensify the color, providing contrast to the naturalistic planting. This garden is designed within what is coming to be called the new wave style from Holland and Germany but with an English twist toward diversity of plant material and color. Taking their cue from nature, new wave designers break up the Edwardian blocks of seven to nine plants (à la Gertrude Jekyll) to create a meadowlike look.

**Foliage color combinations:** While flower color certainly carries this garden at this time of year, you'll see that underneath all those flowers are equally interesting foliage colors and textures that carry just as much visual impact as the flowers. Sweeps of grays and light or dark greens as well as spiky foliage next to broad leaves unify.

**Flower color combinations:** Sandes wants his work "to stimulate every rod and cone in your eye," yet do so in a way that is structured and accessible. Stuart-Smith is after the same thing. His love of color and horticultural complexity is clear, yet this exuberance is carried within a structure. The chartreuse of lady's mantle appears twice down each side of the rill, thereby linking the two sides. Sweeps of yellow-blooming phlomis, gray-leaved stachys, low ornamental grasses, and the mauve globes of *Allium aflatunense* stippled throughout tie this lively garden into a tapestry, the far end of which is held in a lavender bloom of *Nepeta* 'Six Hills Giant', a color sympathetic to the roofing on the barn just below the catmint as well as the distant wheat fields. The visually strong dark green upright yews repeat the dark colors of the nearby woodland, linking the designed garden to the natural world.

# CONTEMPORARY

*Gardeners are driven to give outward form to inner urges, to show what we can do within the artistic world of garden making. And if we garden honestly and from our soul, then our gardens will embody and express who we are.*

Contemporary art is so diverse as to defy definition. Suffice it to say that contemporary art is what is being produced by painters during our lifetime—let's say from 1970 onwards. Because contemporary art includes the upside-down people of Georges Baselitz, the slick neopop of Jeff Koons, Ellsworth Kelly's color field paintings, Frank Stella's shaped canvases, or the personal and political expressions of feminine artists like Judy Chicago, it is impossible to say exactly what this new school of artists as a group points to insofar as art and the garden are concerned.

The point for you as a gardener is to take inspiration from the vast range of experimentation that is presently going on in the world of painting and apply that to your garden making in ways that suit you. Use the Internet. Google such terms as *contemporary painters* and *contemporary American painters,* or narrow the search to *contemporary landscape painters* or *contemporary garden painters.* Then combine that information with Google searches of terms like *contemporary garden styles* or *contemporary Dutch gardens* and see what you get.

To make this exploration of contemporary art specific, I have chosen to look closely at one painting by the contemporary painter Doug Trump, an artist represented by Cynthia Reeves' Contemporary Gallery in Chelsea, New York, New York, *the* geographical center of contemporary art on the East Coast. I could just as easily have chosen any number of artists working today but chose Trump because I think his work has an underlying structure to it that I feel resonates with garden design. Read my analysis of Trump's painting, and whenever you see the word *painting,* replace it with *your garden,* and you'll see what I mean.

# Doug Trump (1950–)

Trump was born in a small town east of Rochester, New York. His mother, a journalist, dabbled in drawing. At age five, he went to the Munson Williams Proctor Institute in Utica to take a ceramics class. In 1956, the family moved to New Jersey, where he attended public schools. At Hackensack High School, he took mechanical drawing classes but no other art courses; he went on to graduate from the University of Pennsylvania in 1972, with a degree in religion and philosophy. He married his wife, Kathleen, a painter who was also involved in medical work. They moved to Boston, and Trump began writing and teaching writing at the Belmont Hill School. They then traveled to Norway and stayed for several months before moving back to Philadelphia, where their son was born in 1973. Trump wrote, studied medicine, then divorced, and moved to Greenfield, Massachusetts, in 1975, where he pumped gas, wrote, worked for the railroad, and one day visited two friends of his who were studying painting at Greenfield Community College; something shifted in him. He began to paint while supporting himself working for the railroad. He moved to Brattleboro, Vermont, in 1980 and then to Kingston, New York, where he established a studio; he painted there for nine years, during which time he started cultivating contacts in New York City. By 1990, he was back in southern Vermont. Curators at the Hood Museum at Dartmouth College asked him to hang his paintings in a regional show. In 1992, he had his first of five shows at the prestigious Berry-Hill Gallery in New York City. In 1995, he had a show at the Chrysler Museum in Norfolk, Virginia, and in 1997 began showing his art through Cynthia Reeves Galleries in Hanover, New Hampshire, and Chelsea, New York City. His work has been part of shows in Santa Fe, New Mexico; Santa Monica, California; San Francisco, California; and Atlanta, Georgia.

*Continued*

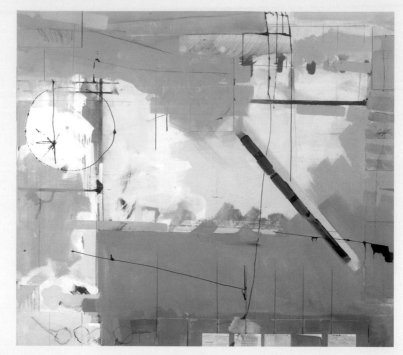

Figure 1.8: Doug Trump, contemporary artist, *In and Out of Philadelphia*, 2001, in a private collection in Philadelphia, Pennsylvania; by permission of the artist and Reeves Contemporary Gallery, New York, New York. Line, in both this painting and in the paths and edges in your garden, directs the movement of your eye as it explores mass, volume, color, and texture.

## Painting

**Movement:** The key to this painting, and perhaps your garden, is movement driven by line, form, and color. Different parts of the painting have different degrees of movement: upper right and lower left are active; upper left and lower right are calm, yet the space between the diagonal bar and the circle are animated and high speed. The contrasting core of the painting is a white motionless void.

**The primary itinerary of the eye:** Your eye is caught by the large green block in the lower-right corner and the five collage pieces of manuscript in the lower-right corner. Your eye then goes to the diagonal bar, which sends your eye off toward the top of the circle, orbits halfway around it, and spins off to return to the lower-right corner. See this itinerary as a path through a garden, one that leads through distinctly different experiences.

**Events along the way:** The upper-right and lower-left corners are "minor dances," as Trump describes them.

**Line as a source of unity:** Unity emanates from line: horizontal, vertical, diagonal, circular. Black, green, and blue-green lines form an open grid that provides the underlying structure of the painting. "Line is this painting's skeleton," says Trump. "Lines shape space."

**Color harmony as another source of unity:** Trump limited the color range to muted greens, grays, whites, blue grays, and browns with accents of orange pink. Trump explains, "Color is not where the action is. Action is in line."

**Variation of mood:** A good painting, like a good garden, offers a broad variety of moods. Notice how quiet areas sit next to busy ones. Trump said, "Quietness allows the events to happen."

Figure 1.8A: *Helter, Skelter,* a garden design by Tony Heywood, a conceptual artist working in London, England; used with permission of the designer. In the hands of an expressive designer, a garden can take on dramatic and unexpected lines, color combinations, and texture contrasts from plants and materials.

Garden

**Movement—the vortex as the organizing principle:** The spiral organizes this design. The blue glass comes shooting in from upper left. The partially buried railing, the boxwood hedge in the upper middle, and the curving steel mirror contribute to this spinning form. The eye of the hurricane of volcanic rock is at once still yet brings with it all the associations of the earth's core.

**The primary itinerary of the eye:** The blue glass panel with sharklike fins draws your eye first. The light-colored boulders then catch your eye and sweep you up to the curving steel mirror and into an even tighter spiral formed at the center of the circle.

**Events along the way:** The quietness of the lower-left corner lies in contrast to the intense movement in the upper right. The lack of movement in the small peastone of the lower left is in high contrast to all that is happening in the upper right: small slates set like fish scales set up a rhythm.

**Sources of unity:** The central vortex is the primary unifying element around which all subordinate elements gather. Brownish peastone used throughout the garden links the parts in a common field. The color green unifies.

**Color harmony:** Put your hand over the blue glass panel and you'll see that the garden has a color harmony: greens, browns, blacks, grays. Only the slightest hint of orange appears in the iron oxide on the surface of the stones. The calm colors only serve to make the blue black of the glass/stone panel more impressive, even ominous.

**Contrasting complex with simple:** The dense, complex, rising circular core of the idea (the space between the buried railing and the concave mirror) is made all the more intense when seen by the adjacent calm areas. Another contrast is between the massive assertive boulders and the little soft green festucas.

## Painting, Garden Design, and Emotion

Many painters have written about how their art is designed to elicit emotion within the viewer, about how they hope their art is a means of communicating what they feel about a subject. (We know about how deeply Vincent van Gogh was disheartened by critical rejection; he sold only one painting, *The Red Vineyard*, in his short lifetime.) In many ways, painters see their works as a means to reaching out to others, of sharing what they see.

We gardeners are similarly motivated. We are driven to give outward form to inner urges, to show what we can do within the artistic world of garden making. And if we garden honestly and from our soul, then our gardens will embody and express who we are. Some of us are flamboyant and romantic, and we garden that way. Others are cool, restrained, and minimalist, while still others are orderly and controlled yet a bit wild within those edges. None of these approaches is better or worse than any other. They are simply certain styles that fit certain people. As you read the following quotations, think about how the words speak for the garden designer as well as the painter.

**Vincent van Gogh** (1853–1890): "Paintings have a life of their own that derives from the painter's soul."

**Eugene Delacroix** (1798–1863), from a journal entry on January 25, 1857: "The main source of interest comes from the soul of the artist, and flows into the soul of the beholder in an irresistible way."

**Camille Pissarro** (1831–1903), in a letter to his son Lucien dated November 20, 1883: "When you put all your soul to a work, all that is noble in you, you cannot fail to find a kindred spirit who understands you."

**George Inness** (1825–1894): "Every artist must, after all, depend on his feelings."

**Paul Cézanne** (1839–1906), in a letter to Emile Bernard, October 23, 1905: "We must render the image of what we see, forgetting everything that existed before us. Which, I believe, must permit the artist to give his entire personality."

**Pierre-Auguste Renoir** (1841–1919), from *My Way of Painting*: "The work of art must seize upon you, wrap you up in yourself, carry you away. It is a means by which the artist conveys his passions; it is the current which he puts forth which sweeps you along in his passion."

**Jacques Villon** (1875–1963): "We paint to discover ourselves, to explain our deepest nature."

**Lyonel Feininger** (1871–1956): "I am incapable of producing without a warm human feeling."

**Andrew Wyeth** (1917– ): My aim is ". . . not to exhibit craft, but rather to submerge it, and make it rightfully the handmaiden of beauty, power, and emotional content."

**Joan Miro** (1893–1983):

Q:  "What do you think is the direction painting ought to take?"

A:  "To rediscover the sources of human feeling."

**Robert Motherwell** (1915–1991): "If a painting does not make human contact, it is nothing."

"*I often see things around me, but for me to want to paint them they must have a particular attraction—what may be called beauty. When I paint them, I try not to lose control of the primary conception; I am weak, and if I let myself go, in a moment I have lost my primary vision, I no longer know where I am going.*"

—PIERRE BONNARD, 1943

## STEP II
# THE RELATIONSHIP BETWEEN HOUSE AND GARDEN

Sometimes paintings don't need any interpretation at all to inspire ideas for garden design. Both French and American impressionists, for example, frequently painted views inside and outside their homes to record those fleeting moments in the life of home and family. Look at the paintings in this chapter with your own house and garden in mind and design ideas may surface.

American impressionist Matilda Browne, for example, painted the garden and view from the side door of fellow painter Clark Voorhees (figure 2.2), just up the street from patron Florence Griswold's house in Old Lyme, Connecticut. French impressionist Claude Monet painted ducks on a tiny pond; in the background is a door to his home in Giverny; Pierre Bonnard painted many views of gardens and interiors looking out at those gardens (figure 2.4). Because these scenes are so familiar, we are all the more struck by their beauty, in part because they focus on subjects we see every day of our lives yet don't take the time to appreciate.

Because the six paintings that follow are realistic and clear in content, I am not going to pair these with garden images but simply let them stand on their own. In and of themselves, they and paintings like them hold specific lessons for garden design. What I *will* do is point out some of the lessons I learned as a garden designer as I looked at these paintings, in hopes that my observations will spur further thought on your part.

# GARDEN AS THE SETTING FOR THE HOUSE

**Trees create an intimate place for the house:** This is the home in which Paul Cézanne grew up and, as an adult, inherited. Where an artist chooses to set up his or her easel determines a great deal about the composition of a painting. Cézanne chose to set his where he could see trees in the foreground, the branches of which overlap the house, thereby making the house feel *within* a grove. He repeated trees in the background—same color, same shape—but of a diminished size because they are at a distance to confirm the link between garden and broader landscape. The house is consequently *of* the landscape, not *on* it. The garden is the setting for the house.

**Color as a means to integrating house, garden, and natural landscape:** The ochre color of the house echoes that of distant hills and fields as well as the yellow ochre of the flat foreground below and above the panel of lawn. House and landscape are one, joined in a color harmony. The geometric wall separating house from lawn is the same color as the house. Dark green shrubs gather by the courtyard of the house, a color repeated in hedges as well as distant trees and shrubs. The blue sky adds brightness to the house through soft contrast.

**Unity—lines in the house generate lines in gardens:** The geometry of the house extends into the geometry of the garden. The lines of the house generate those of walls and steps off the right wing. That geometry extends into the hedge on the right and left. That hedge not only keeps your eye in the picture but also directs it toward the house. The two dark green horizontal edges of lawn run parallel with the ochre wall as well as the walls of the house. Cézanne painted his linear garden with deep affection.

**Pleasing contrast:** The geometry of the house, walls, hedge, and lawn lie in pleasing contrast to the arching branches and the natural forms of trees and foliage in both foreground and background. This gentle contrast makes each more beautiful. Peace settles in.

## Paul Cézanne (1839–1906)

Cézanne was born into a wealthy banking family in Aix-en-Provence in the south of France. His tyrannical father created an oppressive atmosphere within the house and family. It was his childhood friend Emile Zola, who went on to become one of France's great writers, who helped Cézanne free himself from his father's overbearing attitudes. With a small stipend from his father, he went to Paris to study art; his time in the Louvre would change him from a regional painter to one of international stature. In the early 1870s, after years of painting somber, violent, dark paintings, his worked changed forever upon meeting fellow painter Camille Pissarro. He showed Cézanne the world of nature and light and the joys of painting *en plein aire*—in the open. Pissarro pulled him away from his personal demons—his fear of intimacy, his obsession with Wagner's music, his revulsion at being physically touched, for example—and showed him that painting could be a joyous act. Cézanne once wrote, "Art is a harmony parallel to the harmony of nature." American artist Frank DuMond often quoted this. When his parents died, Cézanne inherited the family home Jas de Bouffan (House of the Winds) and its parklike garden, to which he returned. During the last five years of his life, he painted and gardened at his own Les Lauves, where he had a small studio, a secluded half-acre garden at the edge of Aix-en-Provence, and a gardener.

Figure 2.1: Paul Cézanne (1839–1906), *Chestnut Trees and Farmhouse of Jas de Bouffan*, in the collection of the Pushkin Museum of Fine Arts, Moscow, Russia; photo by SCALA/Art Resource, New York. Simplicity leads to strong design. Cézanne paints house, walls, and gravel paths in a limited range of yellow ochres combined with strong black lines so house and land fuse seamlessly. The greens and freer forms of trees contrast pleasingly with the linear house, walls, and paths.

**Overall perspective:** Matilda Browne set up her easel so that the side and roofline of the house gently forms perspective lines that throw your attention out toward the river. This perspective assures a visual relationship between the greater landscape and that of the house.

**Frame a view:** A view is not part of a garden until it has been framed. Browne painted in the dark green tree on the far left of her painting to act with the corner of the yellow house to frame a view of the river; this holds your attention within her painting. That framing directs your eye outward but does not let the spirit of the painting "leak out" to the left. Bonnard does the same in his *The Terrace at Vernon* (figure 2.5).

**Creating a feeling of intimacy and warmth:** Many details in this painting show how Voorhees created welcome near his front door: the sheltering porch with an awning and a rocking chair on it; the detail of planters sitting on the lower stone step; the shutters and trellis on the side of the house; the awning shading the back porch; vines climbing the porch support post; the soft yellow color of the house; the shadows on the lawn that promise the shelter and shade of a nearby tree; the depth of the flowering lively plantings along this wall of the house. There is even a fun-loving evergreen topiary of a bird, one that grew in this spot and perhaps referred to Voorhees' hobby as an amateur ornithologist (and duck hunter).

**Sources of unity:** Browne used many shades and hues of green to knit this painting together. The green of the lawn in sun is the same as the spit of land in the estuary. Blue greens and gray greens appear throughout. There is a simple, unselfconscious way that Browne has approached all elements of this painting. It is not saccharine, but one that sees the simple unadorned beauty of the scene.

## Matilda Browne (1869–1947)

Browne was born in Newark, New Jersey. As a child, she studied under a neighbor, artist Thomas Moran; Frederick Freer, another artist, came from Philadelphia to give her lessons as well. She subsequently studied under a number of others, each with a specialty: flower painting, livestock, and animal painting. After a trip to Europe in the late 1880s, she returned to New York City and began to exhibit her work. In 1889, she studied in Paris under Julian Dupre, one of the great French painters of cattle. She went on to Holland, where she purchased a cow that turned out to be an unwilling model. She lived in Cos Cob, near Greenwich, Connecticut, in the late 1890s. From 1905 to 1906 and periodically between 1911 and 1924, she was the only woman invited to be part of the Old Lyme art colony that gathered around the home of Florence Griswold. In 1918, she married Frederick VanWyck. She exhibited in 1890 in the Salon in Paris, for fifty years at the National Academy of Design, and four times at the Art Institute of Chicago, among many other august art institutions.

Figure 2.2: Matilda Browne (1869–1947), *Clarke Voorhees House*, Florence Griswold Museum, Old Lyme, Connecticut, used by permission of the museum. Browne introduces a few more colors than Cézanne used in house and garden, but not many. The lesson: to create calm, limit colors and textures around your house.

**Overall perspective:** The lines formed by the meeting point between the horizontal floor and ceiling and the vertical walls provide the movement in this painting. Lines of vanishing perspective draw your attention from inside the house out into the landscape, therefore establishing the visual link between the two that is the point of this gentle painting.

**Doorways frame views into the garden:** This is the east-facing front door of the Florence Griswold house in Old Lyme, Connecticut. William Verplanck Birney, like many other East Coast American impressionists of the day, rented a room in her home for years as the art colony there flourished. Here, Birney is expressing his view of the warm relationship between inside and outside, and how this doorway is the point where the inner home and outer garden intersect. This doorway leads to the front porch, where artists often gathered on sunny summer days for high old times. What you see when you open your front door affects how you feel. The view from an open front door is one of the key views from house into garden; it is *the* most important transition between house and garden.

**Color as a means to unifying inside and outside:** Birney is painting on a sunny day when sunlight is slanting through the doorway to illuminate a section of the floor of the front hallway. That light reflects onto the door, providing a vertical and horizontal path of similar light and color. He repeats that color, and hues of it, outside, in the horizontal band of yellow (the road) just behind the base of the tree as well as the yellow sun reflecting off shrubs and meadow grasses in the middle background. The brown in the trunks of the trees is repeated in the furniture. Birney does very little to mark the separation between the floor by the door and exterior surfaces; in fact, the two are visually related through a common color. House and garden are, to his eye, intimately related.

**A note:** The Christmaslike garland festooned in the hallway in midsummer was hung as a remembrance to Allen Talcott, one of the founding members of this art colony who died in 1908, the year Birney painted this picture.

## William Verplanck Birney (1858–1909)

Birney was born in Cincinnati, Ohio. He studied art at the Massachusetts Normal Art School and under Thomas Eakins at the Pennsylvania Academy of Fine Arts. He then went to the Royal Academy in Munich, Germany. Upon his return to the United States, he established a studio in New York City, where he was a member of the art society Salmagundi.

Figure 2.3: William Verplanck Birney (1858–1909), *The Front Hall*, 1908, Florence Griswold Museum, Old Lyme, Connecticut, used with permission from the museum. As Birney did, stand back from your open front door and assess what you see. Your open front door should frame a view into your garden, not a view of cars passing by.

**Seeing through a frame:** Pierre Bonnard emphasizes inside and outside by contrasting the white tablecloth in the lower third of the canvas with the softer greens of the garden outside. The upper two-thirds shows three panes of glass that frame the view as well as the railing on the terrace outside, which forms a secondary frame. Windows become frames for individual paintings within the larger canvas.

**Mood:** Tranquility emanates from this canvas. Bonnard captures that delicate morning moment when the family has awoken, the table is set for breakfast, and the sun is shining on the garden. The soft colors suggest a quiet moment at the beginning of the day. The casual layout of the food on the table, along with the peaceful feeling outside, implies the equanimity with which this family is approaching the day. The setting for this painting was the house at Arcachon, where Bonnard and his wife, Marthe, stayed from October 1930 to April 1931. Marthe appears to the left.

**Structure:** The frames of the window and table give firm structure to this painting. The white tablecloth is the foundation for the painting on which the upper two-thirds rests. The upper part of the painting is divided into five vertical subplots: the woman on the left sitting against the tall curtain; the tall narrow window framing a view of both railing and distant garden; the large central frame; the next narrow vertical frame; the far-right vertical section of curtain.

**A Bonnard quotation:** In a letter to Charles Terrasse, written in 1915, the artist expresses one of the struggles garden designers wrestle with: Which should dominate, color or form? Bonnard wrote: "Certainly I had been carried away by color. I was almost unconsciously sacrificing form to it. But it is true that form exists and that one cannot arbitrarily and indefinitely reduce or transpose it."

## Pierre Bonnard (1867–1947)

Bonnard was born in Fontenay-aux-Roses, a suburb of Paris. His father, Eugene, had a successful career as a civil servant and became Chef de Bureau at the Ministry of War. After attending lycées and graduating, Pierre went on to study art at the Académie Julian to prepare for entrance into the École des Beaux-Arts. His wish to study art was thwarted by his father, who wanted him to study law. He did, but in a desultory way. He passed the bar exam in 1888 but failed to pass the civil service exam. Bonnard's father was a man who was interested in art and loved gardens. But it was his mother, Elisabeth, from a wealthy Alsatian family, and his grandmother who encouraged the young Bonnard. He seemed to gain little from his teachers but a great deal from his fellow painters, especially Toulouse-Lautrec, whom he met in 1891. He left Paris in 1910 for the South of France. In the 1920s, he and others formed the Nabis, a group dedicated to symbolist and spiritual paintings.

Figure 2.4: Pierre Bonnard (1867–1947), *Dining Room Overlooking the Garden (The Breakfast Room)*, 1930–31, the Museum of Modern Art, New York; photograph by the museum and licensed by SCALA/Art Resource, New York; copyright Artists Rights Society, New York/ADAGP, Paris, France. Stand at each window in your house or sit at your dining or breakfast table looking out nearby windows to see what views your windows frame. Key windows frame key viewpoints; make what you see from them beautiful.

# A TERRACE RELATES INSIDE TO OUTSIDE

*Pierre Bonnard juxtaposes complementary colors to add vibrancy to The Terrace at Vernon: blue sky and water, orange-yellow house and orange-ochre field. He then uses the color green in all its variety to knit the picture together.*

**A terrace—half house, half garden:** Pierre Bonnard sets his easel on the terrace, a level built surface that extends the interior floor into the garden. The geometric lavender-blue fence gently encloses the outdoor living space, as does the handrail on the right. These built edges contrast with and thereby heighten the wild untended trees and shrubs painted in many, many greens. Herein lies the central tension of this painting—the balance between untended nature and built structures.

**Holding your eye in a balanced painting:** The yellow-painted corner of the house contains the picture on the left; the large tree contains it on the right. Branches of that same tree provide the space with its leafy sparkling roof. Just a hint of the surface of the terrace provides the base for the painting. The central mass of dark foliage forces your eye to look out to both the right and left of it, toward the two women, the sparkling river, and beyond. The blue sky echoes the river below.

**Establishing scale:** Bonnard includes two women in the picture, one looking away from us as she entices the parrot onto her hand, the other looking toward us. The moment we notice these two figures and the handrail near them, we understand scale.

**Defining depth:** Because we know how big a horse is, when we see those grazing in the distance, bottom right, we understand how wide the river is, how large the distant field is. Comfort and clarity result in that you know where you are in space.

**Color:** Bonnard juxtaposes complementary colors to add vibrancy to this picture: blue sky and water, orange-yellow house and orange-ochre field. He then uses the color green in all its variety to knit the picture together. Blue railing echoes blue water and sky. The ochre house to the left echoes the ochre field to the right, an echo of Cézanne in figure 2.1. Sunlight pervades everything. People and nature are balanced, tranquil.

Figure 2.5: Pierre Bonnard (1867–1947), *The Terrace at Vernon*, 1928, the Kunstammlung Nordrhein-Westfalen Museum, Düsseldorf, Germany; photo credit Bridgeman-Giraudon/Art Resource, New York; copyright Artists Rights Society/ADAGP, Paris, France. Stand at the back door of your house and assess how the life of the inside flows or doesn't flow to the outside. Here, Bonnard is celebrating how a terrace extends the life of the inside of the house to the outside.

# SITTING IN THE GARDEN

**The fleeting moment:** Here, Claude Monet teaches us to see the beauty within a fleeting moment: the child playing next to the luncheon table; his wife and her friend strolling in the garden after lunch; the dappled shade on the gravel path; sunlight hitting flower and foliage to create teeny dots of exploding color; the jaunty hanging of the straw hat on the tree branch. We would all be better gardeners and designers if we took the time to see with Monet's attention to detail.

**Itinerary of the eye:** The placement of the child in the lower left, adjacent to the white tablecloth, shows the way into the picture. Your eye starts there, then follows the path into the sunlight and then to the woman in white, her dress made whiter by its juxtaposition with the nearby black hat band. This strong diagonal between these two lightest areas gives the painting structure and a quiet force. Monet also keeps your eye in the painting at the four corners. The diagonal of the slats of the green bench throws your eye into the bright center, as does the downward slope of the pelargonium mass in the upper left. The women in the upper right face into the painting, as does the boy in the lower left.

**Color and unity:** Four masses of green foliage with red flowers further underpin structure and unity: the fuchsia in the green planter; the mass of pelargoniums just to the left of the planter box; the band of more fuchsias along the foundation of the house; the planting just below the woman in the white dress. By using this limited plant palette (based on theme and variation) and then planting these masses in a similar way, Monet unifies both garden and painting.

**Background:** Monet uses his pink house at Giverny to provide a simple uniform background and balance for all the activity in the foreground and middle ground. Any complex planting, especially a perennial border, benefits from the contrast with a simple backdrop: a hedge, a distant meadow, an adjacent lawn.

## Claude Monet (1840–1926)

Monet was born in Paris, and five years later the family moved to Le Havre in Normandy. His mother was a singer; his father was in the grocery store business and wanted his son to follow in his footsteps, but Monet's interest in art was already apparent. In 1851, at the age of eleven, he went to the secondary school for the arts in Le Havre. By age sixteen, he had met marine artist Eugène Boudin, who had a shop close to his home. Boudin became his mentor and taught him to paint outdoors—*en plein aire*. In 1857, Monet's mother died; he left school and went to live with his aunt. In 1861, he went into military service in Algiers but returned home when he contracted typhoid. He regained his health and began to study art in Paris, where he met Pierre-Auguste Renoir, Frederic Bazille, and Alfred Sisley. Together, they began what would become impressionism.

Figure 2.6: Claude Monet (1840–1926), *Le Dejeuner (Luncheon in the Artist's Garden at Giverny)*, 1873–1874, the Musée d'Orsay, Paris, France; photographed by Erich Lessing/Art Resource, New York. Now walk into your garden, looking for a sitting/gathering place. Monet placed his so he and his family could see the garden from at least one set of windows in the house.

# OTHER PAINTINGS OF THE SAME SUBJECT

It is interesting to compare how various artists treat the same subject. To explore this idea, I chose one painting from this book—Claude Monet's *Le Dejeuner (Luncheon in the Artist's Garden at Giverny)*, figure 2.6—and amassed the list you see below, by no means an exhaustive one, of many other paintings of families gathered in a garden near a house. By going to the Web sites of the museums where these paintings hang, you may find images to compare to that of Monet's. You might also find paintings of comparable subject matter by doing Web searches for subjects like "painting, people, garden," or go to Web sites with art images on them to compare how other artists approach subjects similar to those in the paintings I include in this book.

You will also find a wide range of Web sites with searchable art collections; type in the subheads such as I use throughout this book (Sitting in the Garden, for example), within the sites' search boxes, or visit Web sites from major art museums worldwide, and you will find paintings that show different treatments of the same subject. Comparisons and contrasts between and among them will be instructive for you as a garden designer and as one who appreciates art.

John King: *In The Garden*—Anthony Mitchell Paintings, Nottingham, Great Britain

Maurice Marinot—*Woman Sewing in a Garden*, 1907, Musée d'Art Moderne, Troyes, France

Maurice Marinot—*Woman Reading in the Garden*, Musée Municipal, Cambrai, France

Leon Jamin—*In the Garden*, Galerie Berko, Brussels, Belgium

Henri LeSidaner—*Table in Sunlight in the Garden*, Musée des Beaux-Arts, Nantes, France

Alfred Oliver—*A Tea Party in the Garden*, Anthony Mitchell Paintings, Nottingham, Great Britain

Henri Gaston—*A Cottage and a Heart*, Galerie Berko, Brussels, Belgium

Silvestro Lega—*The Terrace*, 1868, Pinacoteca di Brera, Milan, Italy

Paul Gauguin—*Garden in Vaugirard* or *The Painter's Family in the Garden in Rue Carcel*, 1881, Ny Carlsberg Glyptotek, Copenhagen, Denmark

Telemaco Signorini—*September Morning in Settignano*, 1891, Galleria d'Arte Moderna, Florence, Italy

Giuseppe de Nittis—*Luncheon in the Garden*, 1883, Museo Civico, Barletta, Italy

Max Liebermann—*The Garden Bench*, 1917, Nationalgalerie, Staatliche Museen zu Berlin, Berlin, Germany

Charles Robert Leslie—*Child in His Garden with His Little Horse and Cart*, 1840, Victoria and Albert Museum, London, England

Ferdinand von Wright—*Garden in Haminanlathi*, 1856, Finnish National Art Gallery, Helsinki

Eric Werenskiold—*In Familiar Surroundings*, 1882, Lillehammer Art Museum, Lillehammer, Norway

William Merritt Chase—*The Open Air Breakfast*, 1887, Toledo Museum of Art, Toledo, Ohio

Pierre-Auguste Renoir—*Garden Scene in Brittany*, 1886, Barnes Foundation, Merion, Pennsylvania

Demetrio Cosola—*Garden, Summer*, 1879, Galleria Civica d'Arte Moderna e Contemporanea di Torino, Torino, Italy

Auguste Macke—*Garden Gate*, 1914, Stadtische Galeria in Lenbachhuas, Munich, Germany

Maurice Denis—*The Harvest*, 1896, Kroller-Muller Museum, Otterlo, Netherlands

Pierre Bonnard—*Blue Balcony*, 1910, Courtauld Institute of Art Gallery, London, England

"*To my eyes a garden is a vast painting.*"

—Jacques Delilles (1738–1813), French poet

# OVERALL COMPOSITION

## THE PROCESS

Charles Sprague Sargent, first director of the Arnold Arboretum in Boston, Massachusetts, told Beatrix Farrand, a young student of landscape design, to "look at great landscape paintings, to observe and analyze natural beauty, to travel widely in Europe and see all the gardens she could, and learn from all the great arts as all art is akin."

It was my good fortune to be able to speak with artist Richard Schmid at length about the process he follows when composing and developing a painting. Schmid graciously allowed me to include the four images on pages 71 and 72 that show the development of one of his major still lifes, *The Russian Doll*, so that you can see how a painting develops.

By way of introduction, Richard Schmid, widely regarded as one of the most important portrait and landscape painters working in America today, was born in Chicago, Illinois, in 1934. His initial studies in landscape painting, figure drawing, and anatomy began at the age of twelve and continued into classical techniques under William B. Mosby at the American Academy of Art in Chicago. Mosby was a graduate of the Belgian Royal Academy in Brussels and the Superior Institute in Antwerp. Schmid's studies with him involved working exclusively from life—*alla prima*, or direct painting.

At ceremonies hosted by the American Society of Portrait Artists at the Metropolitan Museum of Art in New York City in 2000, Schmid received the John Singer Sargent Medal for Lifetime Achievement. In 2005, Schmid was presented with the Gold Medal from the Portrait Society of America during their annual portrait conference held in Washington, D.C.

Schmid now lives in New Hampshire with his wife, painter Nancy Guzik. Together they have organized a school in Putney, Vermont, called Putney Painters. Painters (teachers and students) come from across the country to learn from them.

In my conversations with Schmid about the sequence he follows when developing a painting, I was struck with how similar his process is to that of my process as a garden designer. He writes in his book *Alla Prima:*

> The things you do at the start of a painting . . . will determine the entire course of your work. They will make the difference between an achievement and an ordeal. . . . Think about what you intend to do. Think of yourself as being at the start of a beautiful journey with some ordinary realities lying ahead. If it were a real trip, perhaps in a car going across the country, you would want to have maps, credit cards, gas, enough time, and a destination . . . Above all, you must have a route. You must have a *path* to get where you wish to go. Starting a painting starts with the path, with the way in."

The journey is also the way into a garden design. First design the paths, the spines of the garden. They lead from the front and back doors to major destinations: a gazebo or an arbor, a bench or a copse of trees. These primary paths, in concert with secondary paths as well as hedges, walls, and fences, form the big bones and edges of the composition. Then design the winter garden, which is comprised of the smaller bones and ribs of the garden: bed edges, trees, major shrubs, and large-scale perennials such as lasting ornamental grasses. Finally, fill in that framework by designing the content of those beds so that there is detailed and colorful interest during the spring, summer, and fall.

To see this same process in the form of a developing painting, take a look at the next four images; they record the sequence Schmid followed to create *The Russian Doll.* I will add this one caveat from Schmid's *Alla Prima:* "There are times when I have started a work with an end in mind, but then, for one reason or another, as my picture unfolded, it emphatically suggested another direction . . . I always accept that risk and go for it. I'm convinced that at such times my painting is wiser than I am."

## Start with the Primary Path (Figure 3.1)

**Painting:** Schmid told me that a painting is organized by taking "a lot of little visual journeys." You can see in step one of his painting that he began with an S-curve that leads to three blocks of color: one red and two brown at the middle top of the canvas; these are the destination for his primary path, his way in. He then took two subordinate journeys to the right and left of those three blocks of color. This is his early route on the journey in.

**Garden:** Make a scaled drawing of your house and the area you want to garden. Start your design with primary paths, those that lead from the front and back doors into new garden areas. Decide where the destination of those paths will be, just as Schmid did in his three blocks of color at the top of his canvas. Then decide where subordinate paths might lead out from that central destination. Keep lines simple. Rosemary Verey's design in figure 4.1A or our crab apple orchard in figure 5.5A illustrates how main paths lead to subordinate paths to provide underlying structure.

## Clarify the Destination for the Primary Path (Figure 3.2)

**Painting:** Establish exactly what the destination for the primary path will be. As Schmid told me, "The focal point of this painting is highlighted by the juxtaposition of the lightest light against the darkest dark. It is the place with the sharpest edges, the brightest colors, and greatest detail." You will see in step two of *The Russian Doll* that Schmid blocked in the doll and the rectangular tin behind it to establish the destination for your eye along the primary path. That destination is the strongest geometric part of the painting: a rectangular box behind a triangular doll.

Figure 3.1: Richard Schmid, contemporary artist, *The Russian Doll,* a still life, used by permission of the artist, stage one. Schmid used the S-curve to provide the visual way into the painting. The brown and red blobs are its destination. Like Schmid, I start all my garden designs with paths and their destinations.

Figure 3.2: *The Russian Doll,* stage two. Schmid then develops the heart of his painting, the triangular doll in front of the rectilinear box. A geometric arbor, bridge, or pergola might act as the destination in a section of your garden.

Figure 3.3: *The Russian Doll,* stage three. Like a gazebo among your garden of flowering shrubs, the geometry of doll and tin contrasts with the freer forms—the scattered pink and red roses. Secondary points of interest, such as secondary paths and their destinations, emerge in relation to the core image, the doll.

**Garden:** This geometric object in your garden might be a built structure like a gazebo, arbor, or pergola that contrasts against the less well-defined foliage of trees, shrubs, and perennials. That is, the path leads your eye through less well-defined plantings to a clearly defined geometric structure. To see some specific examples, take a closer look at the stainless steel arc in figure 1.8A, the bridge in figure 4.7A, or a sculpture in our garden in figure 4.6A.

## Establish Secondary Paths (Figure 3.3)

**Painting:** With the focal point of his painting established—the Russian doll and the nearby red tin—Schmid then paints the subordinate subjects: a smaller doll to the left, a smaller tin behind it, a scattered bouquet of pink roses and books to the right. He also establishes the quiet base, the foundation of the painting where one's eye rests. Activity gathers in the upper two-thirds; quiet settles in the bottom third.

**Garden:** Set up the main path to the primary sitting area and then run subordinate paths through contrasting yet adjacent areas to provide variety, contrast, and visual stimulation along the way. Your base will be lawn, a solid green surface from which rise the colors, forms, textures, and lines of garden areas and their detailed plants.

## Keep Shapes Simple (Figure 3.4)

**Painting:** Schmid established the focal point of the painting, the Russian doll, by painting her triangular form against the backdrop of the rectangular tin. The simple geometry of this pair contrasts with the non-geometric objects surrounding it. Notice that the S-curve has disappeared, yet its underlying intention remains intact. As Schmid told me, "Don't make the design too obvious. You don't want the design to overwhelm the viewer." Objects that are subordinate to the doll lead your eye to her: the angle of the two books on the right; the ellipse formed by pink roses whirls away from her but then sweeps back like a garland around her; the smaller doll faces her.

**Garden:** The primary focus in your garden should be supported by nearby secondary elements. The destination for your guests, a gazebo at the end of a path in line with your back door, for example, can be reinforced by the way you design the edges of nearby beds. (See our garden in figure 1.2A.) Subordinate objects such as a sundial placed on a pedestal along a path leading to the primary gazebo can draw guests toward the primary destination. See the staddle stone in our spring garden in figure 1.3A.

Figure 3.4: *The Russian Doll*, completion. Every part of the painting—the angle of the books, the layout of the roses—directs your eye toward the doll just as paths lead to key destinations in your garden.

Figure 3.5: Rosemary Ladd, *Hilltop*, 2006, in the author's collection; photograph by John Nopper. Like a garden, a painting is comprised of calm simple passages and complex energized ones.

Examine how you react to the meadow, trees, house, and its setting and then how you react to each part of your garden.

# THE PARTS OF A WHOLE PAINTING, A WHOLE GARDEN

## The Main Point of Interest (Figure 3.5)

**Painting:** Rosemary Ladd, a contemporary painter and student of Richard Schmid's, told me that in *Hilltop* she emphasized the house in a number of ways, all of which are ways the garden designer can throw similar emphasis onto a focal point:

1.  The darkest dark (the stone retaining wall and the patches of dark in the windows) is next to the lightest light (the light green strip above the stone wall, the white of the siding of the house). That stark contrast draws attention to it. (Go back to figure 1.2 to see how Camille Pissarro juxtaposed the edge of the building with the white backdrop in the center of his painting.)

2.  The darkest darks are also near the house in the form of two large tree trunks and the three-stemmed tree.

3.  The sharp-edged geometry of the house, the only geometry in the painting, stands out in contrast to the meadow, the free forms of the trees, and shrubs under them.

4.  The house is drawn with straight lines, unlike the rest of the painting, where nature is almost abstracted.

5.  The color red in the leaves of the Bloodgood maple draws attention, partly because it is the only red in the painting and partly because it is surrounded by green, the complement of red—they are opposite one another on the color wheel.

**Garden:** As garden designers, we can use all five of these methods to make a focal point stand out. We garden around our hundred-year-old weathered garden shed so as to emphasize its triangular gable end and the antique windowpane set into it. Being dark brown, it is the darkest dark and is seen against the lightest light, the sky as well as the gray leaves of a nearby silver willow. A terra-cotta pot planted near one corner of the shed with a large burgundy red coleus echoes the way Ladd used the red-leaved maple in this painting.

## The Strength of Open Space (Figure 3.5)

**Painting:** Concentrated detail in house and trees draws our eye to the main focus of the painting; these more sharply defined elements contrast with the soft, hazy green meadow and its gentle diagonal, which leads our eye from lower left to upper right and then through the trees to the house. This nearly abstract meadow is a soft resting place for the eye. The diagonal emphasized in the light green "path" is the way into the painting; the house, trees, and wall are the destination of that path. As Ladd told me, "What I wanted to do was to create a lot of surface in that meadow and then paint the house like a little jewel there among the trees." The simplicity of this composition is the source of its strength.

**Garden:** The strength of so many successful gardens lies in the fact that there are quiet places for the eye and the body to rest before entering the next complex, densely planted space. (See the quiet deck surrounded by complex planting in figure 4.5A or the bench under oaks in our meadow in figure 5.1A.) Complexity relies on adjacent simplicity for its meaning, just as light relies on shadow for its meaning, just as geometry relies on natural forms for its meaning. Use these pleasing essential contrasts in your garden and it will take on clarity. But if your garden is all perennials, all annuals, all color, or all hard-edged and minimalist, it will lack depth of meaning and emotion.

## Looking Up—Strength in the Unexpected (Figure 3.5)

**Painting:** Landscape painters often set their easels so they paint looking straight ahead or down. Here, Ladd looks up; part of the success of this painting is its unexpected vantage point. One problem with looking up is that the subject of a painting can appear to loom over the viewer, yet that does not happen here. Quite to the contrary, the house is made to feel comfortable; it snuggles within the copse of trees and therefore feels *within* rather than *on* the landscape. The unexpected angle and composition of this painting is not at all self-conscious, as paintings from unexpected angles can be. Ladd told me that the morning she went out to paint this, she had been looking at a book titled *Wyeth at Kuerners,* a book of sketches and paintings by Andrew Wyeth, the master of unexpected vantage points and compositions.

**Garden:** Unexpected angles can bring a garden alive. We once visited the garden of the well-known English garden photographer Andrew Lawson (figure 1.7A is his photograph). He had arranged nine small rectangular beds on a grid set on the diagonal with the house only ten feet away. The strength of this unexpected method of organizing a garden gave it force and strength. The vortex garden in figure 1.8A is filled with unexpected angles, as is the minimalist entry garden in figure 1.5A.

## Creating Unity among Disparate Elements (Figure 3.6)

**Painting:** Kate Gridley set herself the classic task of a still life: joining disparate objects into a balanced, unified whole. In fact, that is *the* task facing every painter and garden designer. Gridley set up her still life to include a table, a lace table cover on which sits a silver bowl containing six pears, a small white porcelain

Figure 3.6: Kate Gridley, contemporary painter, *Gordon's Pears*, 2004, in the author's collection, photograph by John Nopper. The cloth that runs through this composition draws all parts into a relationship with it. Like the main path in your garden, it links parts, in combination with a muted color scheme, into a unified whole. The pewter bowl with pears acts as the center, just as the Russian doll does.

pitcher, a glass jar, and a framed drawing of radishes she had just completed for a book on vegetables, all set against a plaster wall.

**Garden:** As a garden designer, your job is to join trees, shrubs, perennials, lawn, planted pots, built structures such as a gazebo or arbor, fencing, or a bird bath into a unified whole through which paths run. That is, design is the act of relating the parts to the whole.

## Overall Structure (Figure 3.6)

**Painting:** The brown antique table forms the base of this elegant painting, just as the sidewalk does in Childe Hassam's painting (figure 3.8), just as the white tablecloth does in Schmid's painting (figure 3.4).

The gray to brown to purple wall forms the background; the two colors relate. The white cloth runs from the middle left through the objects and then falls off the far-right edge. This creamy white cloth, like a river or path running through a landscape, relates all parts.

**Garden:** The cloth is very much like the main path that runs through your garden. The cloth leads your eye, visually links parts into relationships with it and one another just as the main path through your whole garden or parts of it provides the same links. The cloth, like a well-made path, does not try to take center stage. A well-designed path remains in the service of what it leads from, past, and to. See the path through our spring garden in figure I.3A.

### The Central Focus (Figure 3.6)

**Painting:** The pears in the highly polished silver bowl visually and physically occupy a space just off center. This is the still point in the work; all activity and movement—of the central cloth, the asymmetrically placed lace, the movement of the creamer pointing left, the light playing on the glass jar—are in quiet contrast to the pears in the bowl. Two colors step forward: the white antique lace under the pewter bowl stands out as the clearest high-key white. That lace draws attention to the second color, the yellow-green pears, which, I might add, my brother Peter grew on the family orchard in northwestern Connecticut. The yellow of the pears is further heightened by their green leaves, one of the stronger color contrasts in the painting. The work has a single focus, just as Schmid's does. There is a core of the idea.

**Garden:** Gardens need centers, core ideas, too. Place a terra-cotta urn in the center of a perennial garden behind which is a uniform green hedge and your eye has a clear start to its itinerary. Choose perennials and shrubs to contrast with the color of the terra-cotta urn (blue cornflowers, blue asters, or *Viburnum dentatum* 'Blue Muffin') and your garden will have a visual and physical center. Use the color to draw interest where you want it. See how the designer used the balustrade in figure 4.2A or how we used terra-cotta and a gate in our herb garden in figure 4.10A.

### Overlap Objects to Establish Depth (Figure 3.6)

**Painting:** Another way Gridley created calm unity was to overlap objects. The primary structure of this restrained

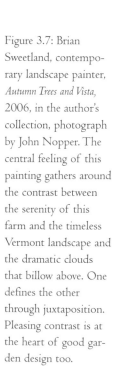

Figure 3.7: Brian Sweetland, contemporary landscape painter, *Autumn Trees and Vista,* 2006, in the author's collection, photograph by John Nopper. The central feeling of this painting gathers around the contrast between the serenity of this farm and the timeless Vermont landscape and the dramatic clouds that billow above. One defines the other through juxtaposition. Pleasing contrast is at the heart of good garden design too.

painting—the table at the base, the creamy white cloth running the length of the painting, the related colors, the simple background—establishes unity that is then underpinned by overlapping objects so that depth and unity result. Overlapping establishes visual relationships.

**Garden:** Overlapping is central to good garden design. When you stand on a path and see white- and blue-flowering perennials overlapping a pink-flowering shrub, you take pleasure in that color combination. When you see orange-, yellow-, and red-flowering perennials against a chartreuse-leaved shrub, you take a different pleasure in this more arresting combination based on overlapping. If, like Gridley, you want a certain combination to stand out, choose muted plants with which to surround the more brightly colored center of attention. Again, look at figure 4.10A as an example of overlapping images in our herb garden entry.

## Objects with Personal Associations (Figure 3.6)

**Painting:** While you, the viewer, may not know that every object in this painting has personal associations, Gridley does. Like your grandmother's birdbath in your garden, that knowledge informs the warmth behind the work. The table, lace, silver bowl, cloth, and jar are all from her grandparents. She grew the radishes and painted them for a book her husband was editing on gardens and cooking. She purchased the creamer when studying art in Florence; it appears in virtually every still life she paints. This painting is a layered story of Gridley's past.

**Garden:** When you place objects with personal associations in your garden, as we have done, those objects take on a special meaning for you and those in the know. Sometimes visitors ask about the piece and learn about the associations but more often they don't. The point is that objects with associations add depth

and character to your garden. See the staddle stone in figure 1.3A, an echo of Mary's past on her family's farm in the Cotswold hills of England.

## Overarching Idea (Figure 3.7)

**Painting:** Brian Sweetland said, "Before I start a painting, I have to decide if it is going to be about atmosphere, texture, color, line, form, mass, or mood. I have spoken over the years with many painters about this idea, and they all agree. There are many abstract elements in a painting, but one of these must take primacy. All the others will be part of the painting, all the others will be important, but by definition, they must play a secondary role to the major element. This painting is about atmosphere, about clouds first and landscape second."

**Garden:** You need to decide what design elements will predominate in your garden or in areas of it. One area might be all about color, another about the mood under trees underplanted with simple groundcovers, another about the motion of ornamental grasses in full sunlight. Color, form, mass, and line in bed edges will all play their roles but remain subordinate to your central idea. For example, the overarching idea for an area of Mount Cuba Gardens in figure 5.3A is the interplay of vertical woodland reflected in horizontal water.

## Sweetland's Sequence in Composing *Autumn Trees and Vista* (Figure 3.7)

### CLOUDS
**Painting:** Sweetland painted clouds first. He wanted to roll the clouds away from the viewer by deepening the tones at the bottom of the clouds using dark-to-light progression to establish depth. The upper-right and -left corners of the painting are dark in contrast to the lighter clouds. As your eye goes down toward the mountain, the clouds recede even further.

**Garden:** Vary the amount of clouds and sky you can see from various parts of your garden to provide a variety of experiences. The sky as the roof over too much of your garden means it has limited variety overhead. On the other hand, certain parts of your garden might afford a remarkable view of clouds. We sit on the bench in our meadow (figure 5.1A) in large part to admire ever-changing clouds.

## HORIZON LINE

**Painting:** Sweetland wanted a feeling of spaciousness, since the painting is about the clouds and the grandeur above the simple farm. The sky pushed the horizon down to about two-fifths above the bottom of the painting.

**Garden:** Create horizon lines with fencing, hedges, or even mixed plantings. You will find that distant or even close views will "sit" on that horizontal line and be clarified. (See the balustrade in figure 4.2A.)

## THE BASE

**Painting:** Sweetland next turned to the base of the painting: the field that runs the full width of the foreground. Time and again painters will include a base, a foundation on which their subject rests. (Thumb through all the paintings in this book and you'll see what I mean.) In this case, the painter positions the hills and farm buildings between the grand sky and this section of field.

**Garden:** Lawn and sky are often the frame for your garden when seen from ground level. Pay attention to that fact when you shape lawn; the simpler the shape, the clearer the adjacent garden appears. Take another look at the rectangular lawn in Cézanne's painting of his home Jas de Bouffan (figure 2.1) or our lawn (figure 1.2A).

## THE MIDDLE DISTANCE

**Painting:** The middle distance shows two long wedge-shaped mountains to the right and left. They each slope toward the center of the painting, where they meet at the central mountain. The dark notes come forward; the grays and blues recede.

**Garden:** Garden areas need a center, a visual anchor that acts like the central mountain in the painting to draw your eye to one dominant subject; once there, your eye can comfortably wander out to subordinate subjects knowing there is a core object to return to. See the birdfeeder in figure 6.8A.

## ITINERARY OF THE EYE

**Painting:** Sweetland anchors the lower-right corner of the painting with the cozy white farmhouse. He painted the house in the painting's highest value color—white—to draw your eye to it. Your interest lingers at this sheltering house and then wanders over to the barns, the hay wagon, then up to the mountain and to the clouds. The white house has its answer in the white clouds. The itinerary of the eye, then, is bottom to top: white house, barn, trailer, mountain, clouds.

**Garden:** Paths create itinerary, and a white bench, arbor, or pergola can help attract the eyes of your visitors to walk toward it. Your garden will have a successful itinerary if your path runs from a consciously chosen starting point and progresses smoothly—with no dead ends and their resulting reversal of direction—through a series of varied yet related experiences that create a variety of emotions and comes to a clear satisfying conclusion.

## THE POINT OF IT ALL

**Painting:** The composition celebrates the grandeur of this natural Vermont scene and the timeless landscape in which the Woods family has lived and farmed for decades. The point of the painting is the harmony with which this farming family and nature coexist.

**Garden:** If you have land around your garden, take an easy-to-carry chair with you one day and walk well

Figure 3.8: Childe Hassam (1859–1935), *At The Florist*, 1889, the Chrysler Museum of Art, Norfolk, Virginia; photographed by and used with permission of the Chrysler Museum. Read the rhythm of this painting from left to right: the base notes in the pavement and wall; the melody in the white wrappings of bouquets and potted plants punctuated by the strong white note of the maid's apron; the high notes of flower color. Your garden has a rhythm too.

away from your garden to a hillside, an open woodland, or some other natural undesigned site and find *the* place for a bench where you can look down over some or all of your house and garden so as to see it in relation to the wider natural world. You, too, may have a spot such as Sweetland found when he set up his easel in this Vermont field.

## Overall Structure: Horizontal Bands, Vertical Accents (Figure 3.8)

**Painting:** (As you read this following text, imagine yourself standing in front of a mixed perennial/ shrub/tree border in a garden.) Childe Hassam painted this frieze-like canvas in 1889. As with the other painters in this chapter, Hassam established the base or foundation—the gray street surface, curbing, and sidewalk—on which the main scene rests. The street and sidewalk set up strong horizontals echoed in the way the paper-wrapped upright pots are drawn in loose bands across the full width of the canvas. The two standing women break that horizontality, as does the tree trunk behind them and the potted standards either side of the tree. This gathering of vertical elements is balanced by the large display case at the back with its own horizontal rows of wrapped flowers.

**Garden:** This elegant painting is a model for lively yet balanced mixed borders of perennials, shrubs, and trees: the green lawn as its setting or foundation; flowering perennials running the length of the border, their color balanced by small trees, potted plants in the border, and a large flowering shrub throwing flowers of similar colors to those of the perennials. In many ways it's what you would see if you were standing on the path looking into Rosemary Verey's plantings at Buscot Park (figure 4.1A).

## Inner Structure, Visual Center (Figure 3.8)

**Painting:** The bourgeois lady in a black jacket and hat stands out in contrast to her servant girl dressed in gray with a white apron and cap. They face left. In the background, behind the flowerpots and in front of the display case, is the florist and two young girls helping her. The two girls face right. Women occupy and give inner structure to the center of the painting and hold it firmly in place.

**Garden:** Inner structure in a perennial garden can be achieved in ways similar to those Hassam used: the repetition of a strong vertical element such as a key shrub with burgundy leaves, in both the foreground and background; the placement of planted terra-cotta pots in the foreground at various places along the front of the border; the use of a hedge, fence, or wall at the back to provide a simple backdrop against which to clearly see the more complex foreground. Look at figure 5.2, for example.

## Unity through Color (Figure 3.8)

**Painting:** On one level, the restrained color gray knits this painting together. It is the color of the street, sidewalk, curbing, the dresses on the florist, and the watering can. The gray-brown color of the wall at the back of the picture combines with the gray street and sidewalk to contain and balance the painting top to bottom. The color white ties the middle together and then uses highlights of reds, whites, yellows, oranges, purples, pinks, and greens to bring vitality. Everything is in balance, yet no element of the painting is static or repetitious.

**Garden:** The designer of mixed borders can learn a lot from this painting: balance verticals and horizontals; establish a simple background (a hedge or fence) and foreground (a monochrome lawn or stone or gravel path) in which to contain the exuberance of color; provide visual centers down the length of the border; use vertical trees and shrubs to provide balance and vitality. Look at a photo of the entry of our herb garden (figure 4.10A) to see how we used dark green as well as shadow to contrast with splashes of red, copper orange, and terra-cotta, all punctuated with vertical gateposts, the uprights for our arbor and the standard weeping peashrubs (*Caragana arborescens* 'Pendula') centered in horizontal boxwood-edged rectangular beds.

# TEN METHODS OF COMPOSITION FOR THE LANDSCAPE PAINTER AND GARDEN DESIGNER

Over the decades, landscape painters have employed tried-and-true methods to compose their paintings. One of the classic books on this subject (Edgar Payne's *Composition of Outdoor Painting*) explores many ways to compose a landscape painting. I have chosen ten of those to illustrate here.

With those ten approaches to composition in mind, artist Janet Fredericks and I walked through the one-and-a-half-acre garden my wife, Mary, and I have been developing these past twenty-five years, looking for examples of how we used these same approaches to compose a landscape painting. We found examples throughout but chose only ten spots in the garden as the basis for the ten illustrations you see on pages 81 through 88.

Following each of the images below, both Janet and I offer a brief analysis of what we each saw, from our different perspectives. We hope these will inspire as you search for ways to compose areas of your garden.

## S-Curve (Figure 3.9)

**The artist:** The arborvitae in the upper-left corner are strong sentinels. They create a wall that contrasts with the finer lines of the wild plums on the right. The hedge in the lower left throws your eye upstream, following the S-curve, sweeping you in. The house and the gap in the hedge act as the destination for the visual journey. Shadows fall on the lawn, appealing to my eye as it travels from shadow to light to shadow. I'm constantly fascinated by how space, shapes, line, and shadow all lend themselves to creating aesthetic pleasure or displeasure. (See Richard Schmid's *The Russian Doll*, figure 3.1, the early stages of which are based on the S-curve.)

**The gardener:** Lawn previously flowed all the way up to the arborvitae hedge on the left. By removing much of the lawn to create the eight-foot-wide S-curve path,

Figure 3.9: Initially, amorphous lawn separated beds to the right and left. We took up excess grass on either side to create an articulate uniformly wide S-curve and suddenly the whole garden picture came together.

Figure 3.10: Here, Mary and I paid close attention when pruning branches to frame a dominant circular frame in the foreground and a subordinate circular frame in the background. Trees and branches direct your eye.

we created a relationship between gardens on either side of that path. The path then draws visitors onto a clearly shaped path that runs between related beds. Hedges in the foreground create a subtle threshold to frame the way in. The glimpse of the peak of the house, and the gateway in the hedge, provide the destination for the S-curve path.

## Circle (Figure 3.10)

**The artist:** My eye goes immediately into the bright area of lawn, then up to the angled birch branch and then left to travel down the branch of the crab apple. The lines on the left keep me focused on the distant meadow and keep me in the picture. My mentor, who studied under the artist Hans Hoffman, told me to always take care of the corners of my paintings, each of which, in this case, is different, each of which plays a different role in developing the itinerary of the eye. (See Silvestro Lega's *The Mistress of the Garden* (figure 4.8.) The central focus of the painting is the woman standing within an open circle.)

**The gardener:** We created an entrance from driveway into garden, the circular motion of which helped us frame the space. The rectilinear hedge contrasts with the natural forms of nearby trees and shrubs, and repeats the straight bed edges in the background. The hedge to the right provides a starting point for the circular motion of the space. You enter from the wide-open driveway and through this enclosed circular portal onto broad lawn. This circle channels and intensifies the space; once through it, your viewpoint expands again to the broad lawn.

## Radiating Lines (Figure 3.11)

**The artist:** This is our Piet Mondrian. He once started painting an apple tree and then began to simplify it to black-outlined blocks of colors, and he discovered his style. These hedges, and their shadows, became abstract forms for me—rectangles upon rectangles on different planes: the lawn, the walls of hedges to the sides, in the middle and background. These geometric shapes radiate toward the sculpture inside the hedged garden. All this geometry clarifies the organic nature of the wild trees as

Figure 3.11: Lines in the form of bed edges, paths, or, in this case, hedges, direct your eye and animate a space. Gaps in hedges, and objects framed by those gaps, allow your eye to travel deeper into space.

well as the shadows on the lawn. The interplay of light and shadow is strong here. (See Paul Cézanne's *Chestnut Trees and Farmhouse of Jas de Bouffan* (figure 2.1) for another example of the use of radiating lines.)

**The gardener:** The garden shown in the drawing of the S-curve leads to this rectilinear space. We purposely created contrast as visitors walked from a space organized by a broad curve to this linear area. Those highly directing radiating lines of hedges and shadows focus on the light within the herb garden, and propel guests into it. Previously, the lawn in this area was shaped like a grand piano, a shape with little logic. When we turned the lawn to a rectangle and planted the matching hedge on the left, we threw more focus onto the entrance into the herb garden, the center of which we marked with the armillary sphere on the pedestal to provide a sense of scale and focus.

## Group Mass (Figure 3.12)

**The artist:** People see things differently. I start by being pulled into the central sculpture. Then my eye flows up the nearest post and across to the right and down to lower right, where I begin to connect the bases of the trunks and sense a circle. The individual posts fuse into a single mass. Others might see the sculpture first and then their eye travels up any one of the posts where their eye could stay high, looking at the wisteria for a long time. The arborvitae is a rocket shape that also keeps your eye up. (See Joseph Stella's *Old Brooklyn Bridge* (figure 4.6) for a related example of how the artist gathers lines held by a single red-flashing light.)

**The gardener:** When we completed planting this garden, we realized it would be enhanced by this vertically strong black locust colonnade. It, along with the circular brick pad, also provided a strong center for the garden. The upright posts pair up to frame many views out into the nearby and distant garden. The sculpture of Jason from Greek mythology echoes our two months on the island of Naxos after Mary and I were first married. We picked up the circular motion of the inner posts in the circle of lawn around the apple tree in the next garden area, which guests visit along our itinerary.

Figure 3.12: Massing locust posts in this section of our garden, and then providing a central focus in the form of the sculpture on a pedestal, defines the meaning of this garden. Climbing vines give purpose to the posts beyond that of design.

## Tunnel (Figure 3.13)

**The artist:** The tunnel is insistent, highly directive; it is also mysterious and strongly suggests transition. It's a threshold where transformations take place. The tunnel pulls your eye deep into space, into what is beyond. And that means that what is beyond, in this case the gazebo, has to be important. But then, the gazebo is also a kind of tunnel. It's a place to pause visually and take a seat. (See John Lee Fitch's *Trout Stream, Green River, Connecticut* (figure 4.2).)

**The gardener:** We always take advantage of transitions in our garden, emphasizing even the slightest change in elevation. They clarify the passage from one space to the next and in so doing make the garden more varied. Years ago, we decided to strongly mark this transition; we took lawn up and planted this purple-leaved beech tunnel and put light-colored peastone underfoot. Guests now move from shade under the nearby apple tree into sun, then into the dense shade of the tunnel, then into sun, then back into the shade of the gazebo; intensity of varied experience results.

## Pattern (Figure 3.14)

**The artist:** As an artist, I think a lot about patterns in the organic natural world. For example, I first see the linear Solomon's Seal in this drawing because of its regularity and arch. The stems of those lead my eye to the contrasting broad hosta leaves. My eye then travels right to the trunk of the tree and then moves down and left to begin again. This picture wouldn't be nearly as interesting without the hosta, which provides a kind of break in the otherwise complex pattern. (See Gustav Klimt's *The Park* (figure 5.6). Klimt turned the foliage of many trees into a vast pattern.)

**The gardener:** Pleasing contrast is at the very heart of garden design: the natural forms of plants next to geometric built structures; broad leaves next to frilly ones; orange flowers next to blue. In this corner of our garden, we contrasted the shapes and forms of plants in order to create a pattern, the hosta being the main player. As gardeners, we need to emphasize the contrast of form and color.

Figure 3.13: Our purple-leaved beech tunnel, like any tunnel, directs people's views and their journey through this part of our garden. The bracing on the gazebo echoes the arc of the tunnel.

Figure 3.14: Artists often use pattern to unify their painting. Here, variegated Solomon's Seal forms a foliar pattern with hostas and ferns to unify this area in our woodland garden.

Figure 3.15: Artists and garden designers use pots, chairs, and benches, all of known size, to help people understand scale. Cover the pot and you'll see how you no longer know how big the trees are. The pot, being so visually strong here, in combination with the gravel path and far-right trees, balance the weight of those trees left of the pot.

## Balance and Scale

**The artist:** Scale can create tension, in this case, between an urn and nearby tree trunks. One helps us understand the size of the other. Scale also causes surprise, as the sculptor Claes Oldenburg explores when he places a thirty-foot-high trowel sculpture in the ground at the entrance to a public garden at the Hoge Veleuwe Sculpture Garden, near Arnhem, in the Netherlands. Balance comes when the shape and size of the urn balances the vertical lines of the wild pear trees. I first see the urn. My eye then travels up any one of the tree trunks and then back down to the urn. Shadows also bring me back to the urn. (See Charles-François Daubigny's *Landscape* (figure 5.3) for an example of how the rowboat establishes scale.)

**The gardener:** We chose to place this urn in this woodsy part of our garden to balance the verticality of the tree trunks, to provide a grounded starting place for the eye in this vertical space. Trees and urn are in a conversation here. We also liked the contrasting shapes of the wild organic nature of this area and the man-made grace and regularity of the urn. Place a finger over the urn and watch this area of the garden lose its focus.

## Three Spot (Figure 3.16)

**The artist:** My eye starts in the lower-left corner and travels between the gap connecting the pots, across the plane of the first of three stones, then is deflected by the left chair and turns right, arcs around the other two chairs, and comes full circle. Because the three chairs and tree are so angular, the pots and the three organically shaped stones form the base for the picture. Things in threes (a pair and one other) create their own natural tension: three equals energy, two equals stasis. There is also the tension between the organic and the built, between small and large. (See the use to which Willard Leroy Metcalf in his *Dogwood Blossoms (No. 1)* (figure 4.5) used boulders to underpin the composition of his painting.)

**The gardener:** We set large stones in a sea of peastone to help create a place. Without those large stones, this

Figure 3.16: Landscape artists sometimes use the three spot to compose their paintings: three boulders, three ships, three mountains. Here, we placed three large boulders on which we set three chairs. Three is a powerful number; it sets up a pair and a single. Tension results. Two or four often establishes stasis.

Figure 3.17: Artists and garden designers often use a point of single interest to provide a visual center around which parts gather. This old apple tree calms the center of a circle of lawn; we planted complex gardens at the lawn's perimeter.

*We always take advantage of transitions in our garden, emphasizing even the slightest change in elevation. They clarify the passage from one space to the next and in so doing make the garden more varied.*

Figure 3.18: Artists often use the triangle as a means to compose an image. Sometimes the triangle is subtle, as you'll see in Frank DuMond's use of the three old fence posts and gates in figure 4.10. Here, the triangular gable ends of our house and garden shed provide a more literal use of the repeated triangle to anchor this garden image.

large area of peastone would lack a center. By setting the chairs on these large stones, we further enhance the feeling of making a place for people. The contrast between the organic shapes of the plants in pots and the planes of the large stones and the geometry of the chairs creates a tension beyond that of the three objects. The eye needs something like the shadows to be pulled further into space.

## Single Interest (Figure 3.17)

**The artist:** When you compose a painting around a central subject, such as this apple tree, you enter the image once and, depending on how you see, your eye explores that one image. Your eye lingers on the tree and branching, and only occasionally does it explore objects in the background. Your eye certainly takes a walk, lingering in the shadows and the vertical trees in the background, but the main center of interest dominates all. (See Amedeo Bocchi's *In The Park* (figure 6.7) and how he focuses on one single subject, the woman sitting on a chair in a garden.)

**The gardener:** I pruned this eighty-year-old apple tree into a grand umbrella shape to display the sculptural uplifting qualities of the trunk and branches. This old tree dominates and simplifies this space and acts in direct contrast to the densely planted gardens that precede and follow it. That is, the tree and its shadows provide a respite, a calming influence that rests your eye before you walk into dense plantings. This tree centers the space, acts as a centering influence on the visitor, and provides a roof over your head.

## Triangle (Figure 3.18)

**The artist:** The shadows that ran across the lawn as I was photographing this part of the Haywards' garden led my eye from lower right toward upper left. Then my eye went through the gap in the hedge and followed the triangle of the gable end of the house across to the triangle formed by the gable end of their garden shed. My eye then slipped down the face of the hedge to start the itinerary again. The two triangles of the gable ends of the barn and shed provide the picture's inner structure. (See Camille Pissarro's *Entée du Village de Voisins* (figure 1.2) and how the space between the hedges in the foreground running back to the horse cart and beyond is a large triangle.)

**The gardener:** As a garden designer, I am always aware of the pleasing contrast between built objects, such as our shed and house, and the natural forms of plants adjacent to them. One clarifies the meaning of the other. Furthermore, the two geometrically shaped hedges act in unison with the two buildings to create pleasing contrast with beds and planted pots near them. Hedges silhouette the natural forms of trees and shrubs. The triangular gable ends of these buildings form strong repeated forms, which unify this part of our garden.

"*Could the histories of all the fine arts be compared, we should find in them many striking analogies.*"

—JOHN CONSTABLE, ENGLISH PAINTER (1776–1837)

# DESIGN PRINCIPLES

*E*lements of design appear daunting. After all, what does it mean to define depth, turn negative space into positive space, and create balance? By looking both at paintings as well as photographs of gardens, I hope that you will be able to more fully understand a few design principles by seeing them used by both garden designers and painters. Divining the relationship between two related images is an engaging way to learn. Of course, the goal of this book is to spur you to action, to help you see design principles in new ways, so you approach the design of your garden with new confidence.

Figure 4.1: Joseph Pierre Birren (1865–1933), *Upalong,* in the collection of and used with permission from the John H. Vanderpoel Art Association, Chicago, Illinois, photographed by Greg Luchow of GL Studios, Blue Island, Illinois. Birren is interested in this approachable welcoming village scene just as you may be interested in creating a simple approachable garden. By setting up his easel at the top of a straight village street—your straight garden path—he is able to see into the heart of this familiar town.

# STRAIGHT PATHS

## Painting

**The destination is known:** When you step onto the beginning of a straight garden path or see a straight visual road as Birren painted, you see the destination ahead. Few mysteries appear. The straight path gives reassuring certainty.

**Light and shadow:** How Birren uses light confirms the approachable nature of this familiar scene. Some people stand in sun, others in shade. Houses cast sheltering shade onto the street, as do trees. The interplay of light and shadow enlivens the surface of the road, just as light and shadow slowly animate your lawn from dawn to dusk.

**Color harmony:** A light pink orange suffuses this scene with warmth and welcome. The orange coats worn by several people in both foreground and background echo the orange roofs. The light greens and yellow greens complement that orange light, giving it vibrancy.

**Itinerary of the eye:** The artist balances the post in the foreground left with the woman in the middle-ground right. Your eye slides effortlessly from post to woman and then deep into the painting. The vanishing perspective lines of street and buildings also carry your eye deep into this accessible quiet town.

**Details humanize the scene:** Every detail Birren paints implies the human scale of this town: the closeness of the house façades to the street; the neighborly gathering of people down the length of the street; the large trees that bespeak the gentle past of the place.

Figure 4.1A: Rosemary Verey's design for a formal garden at Buscot Park, Faringdon, Oxfordshire, United Kingdom, photographed by the author. A wall or door partway along a straight path adds mystery to a straight path; treetops above the wall suggest you'll see a woodland garden when you open the door.

## Garden

**The destination is known:** As with Birren's painting, you know where you're going when you start on this gravel path. And because you roughly know the dimension of most doorways in garden walls, you sense how far away that door is and thus how long the garden is.

**Uniform light, no shadow:** Unlike the street in the Birren painting, which is frozen in time, no shadows fall on this absolutely straight, uniformly wide formal path at noon, when I took this photograph. Shadows will animate this path later.

**Color harmony:** Because it is often overcast in England, the chartreuse leaves from the yellow-leaved black locust (*Robinia pseudoacacia* 'Frisia') and the chartreuse flowers of lady's mantle (*Alchemilla mollis*) provide sunny color to this garden. Those light greens contrast with burgundy foliage throughout.

**Itinerary:** A straight path is insistent. To tone that insistence down, plant in a way that is warm and asymmetrical. If you want to support that formality, plant in a symmetrical, spare, minimalist way.

**Scale:** To make this grand formal walkway feel approachable and comfortable, Verey planted small boxwood hedges on either side of the path and then repeated familiar perennials and small shrubs on both sides of it.

Figure 4.2: John Lee Fitch (1836–1895), *Trout Stream, Green River, Connecticut,* 1880, compliments of and photographed by the Cooley Gallery, Old Lyme, Connecticut. Choosing this tunnel-like setting to paint enables Fitch to create depth in his painting, as would a tunnel in your garden. (See figure 3.13 for a tunnel in our garden.)

# THE TUNNEL

## Painting

**Style:** Fitch, who worked in the Northeast, was a master of forest interiors. He painted in a highly intricate and representational style, where even veins on leaves are visible. Here, he is celebrating the deep simple beauty of this woodland stream.

**Structure is itinerary:** Fitch used the classic tunnel to compose his painting (see figure 3.13). Your eye is shown exactly where to go: you start in the foreground with the fisherman and travel deep upstream, drawn by the light color of the boulders on either side of the stream and the brightening of the water. The fisherman's rod, as well as his attention directed upstream toward a trout pool, literally points the way.

**Scale:** Painters (and gardeners) use various approaches to help viewers understand the size of objects. One approach is to introduce an object of universally known size into the picture—a bench, chair, table, or, in this case, a person. By introducing the fisherman, albeit in browns that recede, the viewer can understand through comparison the size of trees, boulders, stream—everything.

**Balance:** By its very nature, the tunnel is balanced left to right. Fitch enlivens what could have been a static symmetrical painting by using dark pigments to render the forest on the right while using lighter pigments to suggest the meadow in the lower left.

**Defining depth:** Fitch achieves depth using a number of devices. One is to show the boulders in the foreground, middle, and background, diminishing in size as you look deeper into the painting. Another is to show the white water as it tumbles over boulders in the lower-left corner, the white waterfalls in the center, and then at various points upstream. Yet another is the misty treatment of the meadow to the left and the far distant trees you can barely discern.

Figure 4.2A: The Birch Allée at Stan Hywet Gardens in Akron, Ohio, photographed by the author. Allées form irresistible tunnels that frame views. Tunnels draw you down their length; overarching branches compress the view.

## Garden

**Style:** The allée goes deep into garden history. Allées often end at a destination that is visible at the outset.

**The structure:** An allée, in this case of white birch trees underplanted with periwinkle (*Vinca minor*), by its very nature forms a symmetrical tunnel, drawing your eye down its length. This two-hundred-foot-long tunnel ends at a cast-stone balustrade on which you rest your hands as you look out over distant ravines and woodland.

**The itinerary of the eye:** An allée is insistent, assertive, and dramatic. Only as you walk down its length do you see subordinate side paths that go off to right and left, into other areas of the garden. This allée acts as the spine of a garden, with paths off it acting like ribs.

**Pleasing contrast:** There are several contrasts at work here that make this view appealing. First is the feeling of comforting enclosure as you walk between the rows of smaller-scale birch trees (as opposed to imposing oaks); that feeling of being *within* is then released as you come out into the open. Second, filtered light within the allée is followed by the brilliant sunshine when you arrive at the railing. Third, you see adjacent gardens through the trunks of the birches followed by an expansive uninterrupted view into distant woodland at the end of the allée: closed/open, shady/sunny, inside/outside.

Figure 4.3: Henri Matisse (1869–1954), *The Luxembourg Garden*, 1901, the Hermitage, St. Petersburg, Russia, photograph by SCALA/ Art Resource, New York, New York, © 2008 Succession H. Matisse, Paris/Artists Rights Society, New York, New York. Curiosity as to what's around the bend in a path draws us forward irresistibly. Make a conscious decision as to straight or curving paths in your garden; they offer very different experiences.

# CURVING PATHS

## Painting

**Destination unknown:** A path with an end that curves out of sight builds mystery and suspense into a painting and garden. Matisse uses this strong curve that runs from lower left to middle right to attract your eye. That strong purple-yellow road is at the core of the picture; all parts relate to it.

**Composition:** Matisse used this strong S-curve (see figure 3.9) from lower left to middle right to anchor the composition of ovals, mounds, blocks, and patches, each in pleasing contrast to one another through color and shape (see figures 3.1 and 3.2).

**Degrees of insistence:** While it is clear that your eye is meant to start at lower left and follow the path into the painting, Matisse has fused path and plantings through color so the path does not stand out in stark contrast. When you choose materials for your garden, choose those that don't contrast too sharply with nearby plants.

**Color:** Pay attention to how light changes in your garden minute by minute as you walk down a path. Here, light flows into the painting from right to left, creating two bands of yellow that contrast with the shaded portions of the path, thereby drawing attention to that central path. Dark greens hold your eye and, through contrast, brighter colors are intensified.

Figure 4.3A: A Joan Kropf design for a hillside garden in Eugene, Oregon, photo by Robin Cushman. What you see from the top or bottom of a set of steps should be commensurate with the nature of those steps.

## Garden

**Destination unclear:** As you stand at the base of these curving steps, you see only a few hints as to their destination. As Dan Kiley, the late and eminent landscape architect, once told me, "The curving path leads to the mystery beyond."

**Composition:** There is a strong lower-right to upper-left curve to the steps that sweeps you up and around. The hint of the teak chair, the curve's destination, shows there is a comfortable flat area up there from which to look down on the garden. The flat-topped wall provides the garden picture with a base. By sloping rather then stepping the top of the wall, the designer emphasizes the sweep and curve of the steps.

**Degrees of insistence:** A straight or curving path planted on both sides requires that once you start up the path, you have to complete the journey. Here, Kropf provides an alternative—the gravel path at the base of the retaining wall. This option reduces the degree of insistence offered by the stone steps.

**Color:** The hard-edged dark browns and grays of the stone walls contrast with the chartreuse, yellows, and wide variety of grays. The brown and aged terra-cotta pots sitting on the steps echo the color of the adjacent wall. Both stand in brilliant contrast to the light green moss on the steps.

Figure 4.4: Jean Hans Arp (1888–1966), *Large Drawing*, 1917, the Musée National d'Art Moderne, Centre Georges Pompidou, Paris, France, photographed by CNAC/MNAM/Dist. Reunion des Musées Nationaux/Art Resource, New York, New York, photographer Phillipe Migeat, © 2008 Artists Rights Society, NY/VG Bild-Kunst, Bonn, Germany. A balance between positive and negative space—between objects and the apparent void between them—means the art, or the garden, is balanced.

# RELATED CURVES

## Painting

**Positive and negative space in balance:** Look first at the black spaces (positive space) as the subject of the painting, then switch and look at the creamy-white spaces (negative space) as the subject. Both are of equal importance to this work and, in a more complex way, to all painting. Artists shape the main subjects of their paintings—trees, a bridge, people, a horse and wagon, women on a terrace—with an eye simultaneous to the shape of the space between those subjects. Both should be in balance.

**Hierarchy:** There is one large black shape anchored in the lower-right corner that stretches left as well as upward. That vaguely right-angled shape is answered by a subordinate yet similar shape in the upper-left corner. These two main shapes frame all others. Arp established a hierarchy.

**The way in:** There are three ways into this mazelike drawing: the gap between the two largest shapes in the upper right; the two gaps on either side of the blocky shape in the lower left.

**Two enclosed spaces:** If you look at the creamy-white spaces as paths and the black spaces as garden beds, you can gain access to all but two interior spaces: one is shaped like a rectangle, the other is just to its right.

Figure 4.4A: Roberto Burle Marx (1909–1994)—*Garden Design Project for Beach House for Mr. and Mrs. Burton Tremaine, Santa Barbara, California*—site plan, the Museum of Modern Art, New York, New York; licensed by SCALA/Art Resource, New York, New York. Choose when to curve beds, when to make beds linear. Appropriate variety is the key. And like Burle Marx, make all curves relate to one another.

## Site Plan

**Positive and negative space in balance:** In this overall plan, all curves relate, including house, pool, driveways, planted beds, garden paths—everything. The shapes between those curves are pleasing and in proportion. One of the biggest problems in residential garden design today is that home gardeners give shape to their beds (positive space) while paying little or no attention to the resulting shape of the lawn (negative space) between those beds. Shape that lawn in relation to the beds, as Burle Marx does, and you'll render negative space positive.

**Hierarchy:** The light green area is lawn, in many places planted with trees and shrubs. Look just at the light green around the perimeter of the drawing; it's the primary curvilinear frame of this garden and is at the top of the hierarchy by virtue of its size and its role of enclosure. The secondary spaces are the two large interior areas of lawn framed by white paths and the driveway that comes in at the left of the drawing and leads to the blue garage. The tertiary spaces are two rectilinear lawn panels framed by brick paths between blue house and garage. This hierarchy might help you to establish your own hierarchy of lawn areas.

Figure 4.5: Willard Leroy Metcalf (1858–1925), *Dogwood Blossoms (No. 1)*, 1906, in the collection of and used with permission from the Florence Griswold Museum, Old Lyme, Connecticut. Pay close attention to the nature of "shade throw" by different species of trees. Oaks throw dense shade, and, in early spring, as you see here, dogwoods throw diaphanous shade.

# LIGHT: DAPPLED SHADE

## Painting

**Light:** Metcalf explores how light filtering down through the still-small leaves of early spring breaks up into tiny dots on the ground. The result is that everything, even massive granite boulders, shimmer and feel as light as air. The white dots throughout the painting—on the ground at the bottom of the painting, on the kneeling woman's back, on the white petals of the blooming dogwood tree—unify the piece. Successful art appears effortless.

**The overarching idea:** Metcalf holds true to a single idea: the effect of light on the landscape. This single idea drives every decision he made. The two main boulders provide a foundation, a grounding for this airy study. The tree trunks provide structure and vertical movement.

The two women and the blooming dogwood tree provide the focal point, yet over everything is the light, the shimmering light.

**Linking foreground to background:** Boulders big and small stitch foreground, middle ground, and background together. The large boulder in the lower left keeps your eye in the painting. The big one to its right sends your eye to the left, to a smaller boulder, then your eye catches on three smaller boulders upward and to the right. Two are in dappled shade; one is in full sun. Just as with any repeated plant or material in a garden, these repeated boulders unify shimmering woodland and sunlit meadow while also drawing your eye deep into the painting.

Figure 4.5A: Honeylocust trees and a deck in garden designer Carol Mercer's garden, Easthampton, New York, photographed by the author. From spring to fall, honeylocusts throw enlivening shade onto any surface.

## Garden

**The play of light on a deck or other uniform surface:** Honeylocusts are particularly good trees to plant right in or near a deck or stone patio. Shadows caused by leaf and branch fall on those uniform surfaces to create ever-changing patterns; wind in the trees animate those shadows. Of shadows cast by trees, Graham Stuart Thomas, English garden writer and designer, wrote in *Art of Planting:* "Wherever possible a tree should be placed so that it casts its shade across the flat lawn in the morning and evening. The dark shadow moving across the lawn as the day passes is a magical addition to a garden view."

**The interplay of horizontal and vertical:** The pleasing contrast between the vertical house and trees in combination with the horizontality of deck and steps is the big idea that drives many of Mercer's choices.

**People like to see big views from little places:** When sitting on this deck and looking to the left, you look out from under the branches of the trees to the nearby swimming pool, a vast expanse of lawn, and an estuary coming in off the Atlantic Ocean in the background. Seeing that big view from this cozy space is appealing in its contrast.

**Accents:** Planted pots and flowering shrubs and perennials provide accents of color to spark an otherwise calm study in graying cedar and lichen-mottled tree trunks. Sylvia Crowe, a garden design historian, wrote in *Garden Design* that planted pots and sculptures "are humanizers by which man projects his personality and love of creation into the realm of nature."

Figure 4.6: Joseph Stella (1880–1946), *Old Brooklyn Bridge*, 1941, in the collection of and used with permission from the Museum of Fine Arts, Boston, Massachusetts. If you have a busy-looking garden, you need to build strong visual centers, as Stella did here with the red light, to help give your visitors a strong still point from which to start their visual journey.

# FOCAL POINTS

## Painting

**A starting point for the eye:** The problem for Stella was to give viewers a starting point from which to unravel the complexity of this painting. He was interested in images of industrial America, and here he is recording his impression of following a fire truck crossing the Brooklyn Bridge. The red circle on which sits the diamond-shaped light first draws your eye. Stella then uses strong diagonals that work from lower left and right to draw us deeper into his painting. The inner or secondary goal for your eye lies directly above the red light: one of the stone support towers from which hang suspension cables. But it is the red light that provides a still point in the midst of frenetic lines. As Jean Baptiste Camille Corot (1796–1875) wrote, "In a painting there is always a luminous point; but this point must be unique. You may place it where you wish . . ."

**Movement:** The subject of this painting is the movement of the city in general and the linear elements of a vast suspension bridge in particular. Even when standing still on the Brooklyn Bridge, one would stand in awe of the complexity of the cables as they create a supporting web. Then combine that complexity with movement, especially that of a speeding fire truck, and you have a cacophony of line and mass. It is this complex movement through space and line that Stella captures.

Figure 4.6A: *Jason of the Argonauts* in the author's garden, photographed by Jerry Pavia. Complex gardens need still points. Garden sculptures, especially those that suggest calm, are central in establishing a garden's emotional, and sometimes physical, center.

## Garden

**A starting point for the eye:** When we first built this rustic pergola and the four-quadrant garden around it, we knew we were creating a complex visual experience for our visitors. To anchor the center of this densely planted garden, we placed this sculpture of *Jason of the Argonauts* on a pedestal. When visitors walk into this area, their eyes go immediately to the sculpture, then out to the frames created by uprights and crosspieces in the pergola and then into the dense plantings of trees, shrubs, and perennials (figure 3.12). Jason is our still point, our visual anchor. As with so many paintings, our focal point is heightened by any number of principles employed by painters: the sculpture is the lightest light seen against the darkest dark (the trunk of the old apple tree in the background); it has clear edges; it is a man-made object surrounded by growing plants.

**Movement:** As in Stella's painting, movement is everywhere in this garden: in the horizontal and vertical lines of the black locust uprights and crosspieces; in the vines climbing those uprights; in flowering perennials and shrubs throughout this garden; in the ornamental grasses that move in the wind. In both painting and garden, all lines overhead and to the sides and shooting out in all directions make you feel you are within that movement, yet the focal point provides reassurance and a visual still point.

Figure 4.7 Paul Cézanne (1839–1906), *Bridge Over a Pond*, 1895–1898, in the collection of the Pushkin Museum of Fine Arts, Moscow, Russia, photo by Erich Lessing/Art Resource, New York, New York. This geometric bridge helps us better understand the contrasting natural lines of trees and their reflections.

# MAN-MADE STRUCTURES CONTRASTING WITH PLANTS

## Painting

**Contrasting Geometric and Natural Forms:** The bridge, like any built structure in your garden, acts on many levels in this painting:

1. The black bridge with white highlights acts as the center of the viewer's focus, the beginning of the visual itinerary.

2. The black bridge anchors and solidifies the picture. It provides essential visual weight to an otherwise ethereal painting.

3. Cézanne painted the foliage in such a way that it overlaps portions of the bridge, thereby establishing depth. This overlapping, along with Cézanne's color choice and brushstrokes, integrates bridge, water, and foliage.

4. The railing along the sides of the deck of the bridge establish a sense of scale.

5. The bridge makes the whole scene accessible to the walker and viewer. The bridge is the way into this painting, into this shimmering pattern of color.

**Releasing the painting into the atmosphere:** In paintings, as well as gardens, there are times when you want to release energy into the sky (figure 3.7). Cézanne does this in the upper-right corner, where he paints the gray blue sky and not more foliage. He releases the concentrated energy of the painting. If you create a garden in unremitting sun or shade, the mood may become too concentrated. Vary the amounts of each.

**Take advantage of the ability of water to reflect light:** Here, Cézanne is clearly interested in the way the mass of foliage held in the air is reflected on the surface of the water. This quintessential fascination with light on the part of the impressionists is a good lesson to learn and can be built into your garden.

Figure 4.7A: A Robin Cushman photograph of a garden designed by Fujitaro Kubota in Seattle, Washington. The color we paint built objects in our garden determines the amount of visual punch they have.

## Garden

**A man-made object contrasts with nature:** As with Cézanne's bridge, you understand the bridge and its geometry by comparing it to the natural forms of the plants and vice versa. You also understand the difference between the two through the complementary colors red and green.

**Visual centers:** The bridge acts as the visual (and dramatic) center of this garden. Its central role is only challenged when nearby rhododendrons are in bloom.

**Itinerary:** Even though you can't see the path, the highly visible bridge offers the promise that all parts of this garden are accessible. As with Cézanne's painting, you can inhabit this bridge, and Cézanne's, in your imagination. Without the bridges, both painting and garden feel inaccessible.

**Motion:** The arched bridge implies motion, acting as both a visual path for the eye and the body.

**Bridge as permanence:** The bridge remains solid and unchanging while the surface of the water and the foliage in the trees move and change. The flowering shrubs, too, change from day to day, yet the bridge remains, unchanging in its solid geometry.

Figure 4.8: Silvestro Lega (1826–1895), *The Mistress of the Garden,* in the collection of the Galleria d'Arte Moderna, Florence, Italy, photo credit SCALA/Art Resource, New York, New York. Pruning an opening in the branches of trees and shrubs is a simple, effective way to frame a view.

# THE OUTLOOK

## Painting

**Framing a view:** Lega creates a circle of branch and foliage around this view to frame it, to make those distant hills a part of this garden. (See figure 3.10 for another example.)

**Positive and negative space:** Painters make choices as to what to include, what to exclude from an existing scene. The painter here uses the trunks and branches of the trees on the right to bring your eye down to the figure of the woman. Even the negative space—the spaces between the branches—takes on shapes that draw your eye down toward the woman. The branches on the far-left tree direct your eye into the painting and toward its main subject—the outlook.

**Light and dark:** The white dog plays its role in drawing your eye to the outlook. Place a finger over the dog and you will see the painting change. The white of the dog so close to the dark coat of the gentleman walking up the hill draws your eye and sends it up and out to distant hills.

**Color:** The darkest dark—the woman's bodice and the trim on her hat—contrasts with the lightest light—the sky—to draw your eye to this key point in the painting. The dark brown trunks of the trees set lines in motion, animating an otherwise still scene, the stillness emphasized by the sleeping dog.

**Composition:** The beige gravel path and green verge of it form the foundation of the painting. The shrub on the left and the fence on the right balance one another and hold your eye. The resting dog, standing woman, and the foliage of both shrubs form a large central circle just off center in the painting and form the subject of the painting.

Figure 4.8A: An allée garden gate in the Helen Woodward Garden, Eugene, Oregon, photograph by Robin Cushman. A threshold, that point where you leave garden A and enter garden B, is a spot that deserves to be marked by an arbor that will frame a view.

## Garden

**Framing a view:** In her garden in Eugene, Oregon, Woodward framed the view not only of her garden but also the distant hills in much the same way Lega did. The gate, like the painter's fence, brings a contrasting man-made object into play as part of the frame. Like the painter, Woodward frames the outlook from above by suspending wisteria and roses on an arbor so as to concentrate and tightly frame the view of the nearby garden and distant landscape. A vista is a framed view.

**Positive and negative space:** The beautifully designed gate is a fine example of positive and negative space in harmony. Notice the voids between the filigree and vertical bars are also beautifully proportioned and consciously shaped.

**Color:** The creamy-pink roses on the foreground echo colors within the garden in the background, just as the splashes of light between the branches and foliage in Lega's painting link foreground to background.

**Composition:** The controlled verticality of the arbor and the horizontality of the gate and fence contrast with the horizontal green swath of lawn that draws your eye in.

Figure 4.9: Henri Rousseau (1844–1910) *Le Douanier (The Dream)*, 1910, in the collection of the Museum of Modern Art, New York, New York, photo credit MOMA, licensed by SCALA/Art Resource, New York, New York. Pleasing contrast is one of the primary elements of garden design. Juxtaposing plants with contrasting foliage helps define the nature of each and every plant in your garden.

# CONTRASTING TEXTURES AND COLORS

## Painting

**Foliage contrasts:** Rousseau contrasts textures across the canvas so that each stands out in contrast to those nearby. The primary contrast, of course, is between the curvaceous body of the Victorian dreamer and the straplike and pointed jungle leaves. The sword-shaped foliage of the white-variegated sansevieria in the lower right contrasts with the round lotus leaves just above them; big broad leaves in the upper center contrast with the finer leaves of the palm in which the orange-breasted bird perches.

**Color contrasts:** Rousseau highlighted the main focus of this painting, the reclining woman, using two methods: first, he places the woman's skin tones against the dark red velvet couch. Second, he contrasts the linearity of the back of the couch with the wild, pointed natural forms of the jungle to make it and her stand out. This is her dream, one punctuated by the sounds of the enchanter's flute. Color contrasts proliferate throughout the jungle: orange fruits growing on the gray-green palm tree; the white-billed orange bird and the beige orange faces of the two lions; the orange snake; the gray elephant and brown monkey; the pink and blue lotus flowers dancing across the middle of the canvas against the green backdrop; the surrealism of a white moon in a blue sky. All colors are knitted together in a scrim of gently contrasting greens.

Figure 4.9A: The garden of Sybile Kreutzberger and Pamela Schwerdt, Gloucestershire, United Kingdom, photograph by the author. The gentle contrast between shorn and natural shrubs, between foliage colors, shapes, and textures clarifies the meaning of this refined garden.

## Garden

**Foliage contrasts:** You can see textural contrast at work in this photo of a section of the Kreutzberger-Schwerdt garden. The yellow-white variegation of the iris in the lower right contrasts firmly with the dark green shorn boxwood. At the same time, the iris leaf contrasts with that of the ground-hugging *Lysimachia nummularia* 'Aurea' yet echoes the yellow-green leaf of the iris. Every plant gains its meaning from the contrast with its neighbors.

**Flower color contrast:** One of the more complex challenges in garden design is to create color combinations based on the color of blooms on plants that flower simultaneously. As Gertrude Jekyll, the great early-twentieth-century British garden designer, said, "Planting is like painting a landscape with living things." Here, Kreutzberger and Schwerdt rely not only on simultaneous bloom but also on a variety of foliage colors and textures to enliven this garden.

Figure 4.10: Frank Vincent DuMond (1865–1951), *Top of the Hill*, 1906, in the collection of and used by permission from the Florence Griswold Museum, Old Lyme, Connecticut. Entry points and thresholds deserve special attention. Define how they move people from shade to sun or from densely planted to simply planted areas, from narrow to broad.

# CREATING ENTRANCES, TRANSITIONS, AND EDGES

## Painting

**Points of transition:** Any painter or garden designer has to provide a way into his or her work, and that way in is often marked by an important transition point. The entry here is framed on the left by dark green shrubs, a portion of stone wall, and the open gate attached to the fencepost, a post answered on the right by another that leans.

**Outer edges:** The base of the painting is the shady meadow at the bottom; the dark green shrubs and gate keep your eye in the painting to the left, just as the leaning fencepost and similarly leaning apple tree above it keep your eye in the painting to the right. The overarching branches of the largely unseen tree hold your eye at the top.

**Inner edges:** The most important inner edge is the diagonal that starts in the lower left and continues in the form of the open gate to the lighter yellow path that leads your eye into the painting. Another inner edge is subtler. The gate and its post on the left form the base of a triangle with the fencepost on the right. The apex of that triangle is formed by two leaning posts in the middle ground.

**Unity:** As with good garden design, DuMond establishes unity through choosing a limited color range. This is a study in greens, yellow greens, and blue grays. The overall structure of the painting is three roughly horizontal bands: the first meadow before the gate; the second, after the gate; the third, the distant trees and sky.

**Mood:** You can feel the peace DuMond must have felt as he worked on this painting in the summer of 1906. Here, looking up at Grassy Hill in Old Lyme, Connecticut, less than a hundred miles from a burgeoning New York City, he, like so many impressionists, was looking back at a rural idyll and capturing how the transitory light fell on this timeless scene.

Figure 4.10A: The entrance to the author's herb garden, photograph by Richard Brown. Pleasing contrasts generated the design of this entry: shaded narrow entry versus sunny open interior; dark green foliage at the entry, light gray greens inside; great slabs of stone at the entry, three-eighths-inch peastone inside.

## Garden

**Points of transition:** We marked this important point of transition in many ways, just as DuMond did: one walks through a narrow shaded space into an open sunny space; the gate emphasizes entry; when one steps on the peastone, it makes a crunching sound underfoot, a sound that underpins change.

**Outer edges:** We form edges in different ways: to the east, the arborvitae (*Thuja occidentalis* 'Smaragd') you see in the background; to the north and south, *Viburnum prunifolium* hedges, the end of which you see to the left; to the west, the arbor and garden shed.

**Inner edges:** All lines are parallel or perpendicular to the garden shed and thus to one another. We planted low boxwood hedges to create the edges of the four quadrants.

**Unity:** All lines are parallel or perpendicular to one another and to the garden shed that anchors this garden area. They form a unifying grid in which we planted herbs informally. Camille Pissarro wrote in a letter dated July 5, 1883: "Strive for simplicity, for the essential lines."

**Mood:** The informal feeling created by the planting style is kept in bounds by the linearity of the traditional four-quadrant garden. Materials such as the irregular stepping-stones and peastone without steel or wooden edging and the antique watering can create a relaxed mood.

In the intimate and humanized landscape, trees become the great-est single element linking us visually and emotionally with our surroundings. We can allow a tree to become a part of us. It's no wonder that when we first think of a garden we think of a tree.

—THOMAS CHURCH, CALIFORNIA-BASED
LANDSCAPE ARCHITECT (1902–1978),
*GARDENS ARE FOR PEOPLE*

# ROLES TREES PLAY
# IN THE GARDEN

T rees are the largest plants in your garden. They contribute height, breadth, stature, and magnificent silhouettes against the sky, as well as foliage texture and color, especially in autumn. They create shady places for people sitting under them in the warm months, and, in northern zones, they hold snow in dramatic ways in the winter months. A copse of trees creates its own little world, separate and different from more cultivated, tended gardens. Mature trees contain the past of the place in them and often conjure up childhood memories. Every time I see the apple tree in our garden (figure 3.17) I am reminded of the apple trees that comprised the orchard I grew up on in northwestern Connecticut. Well pruned, trees are living sculptures; their branches reach up and out, crisscrossing one another and casting ever-changing shadows on the ground as the earth rotates.

The English say that we plant trees for our grandchildren. I know what they mean; a hundred-year-old beech or oak has a stature that only comes with a century behind it. But having said that, Mary and I marvel at the pace at which our *Sorbus alnifolia*, *Acer triflorum*, *Maackia amurensis*, *Stewartia pseudocamellia*, *Cladrastis kentukea*, and *Syringa reticulata* have grown in the few short years since we planted them. Trees grow. Get planting those trees today. Don't dawdle. They add so very much to a garden. Celia Thaxter, the subject of Childe Hassam's painting (figure 1.3), wrote in *An Island Garden:* "Someone has said, speaking of a tree, 'What an immense amount of vitally organized material has been gathered together! It is God's own architecture.'"

To help you understand some of the aesthetic roles trees play in the garden, I have chosen seven pairs of images that will help you see at least seven ways in which trees contribute to the life of your garden and how painters have incorporated them into some of their most beautiful work. Your own research into paintings and garden design will turn up countless other uses for trees, the largest plants on earth.

Figure 5.1: Claude Monet (1840–1926), *Summer*, 1874, in the collection of the Nationalgalerie, Staatliche Museen zu Berlin, Berlin, Germany; photo credit Bildarchiv Preussischer Kulturbesitz/Art Resource, New York, New York. Choose trees, the foliage of which either complements or contrasts with the colors of the grasses and wildflowers in the meadow.

# VERTICAL TREES IN A HORIZONTAL LANDSCAPE

## Painting

**Tall trees in a meadow:** Vertical trees in horizontal landscapes create beauty through pleasing contrast. Notice the five horizontal lines here: the dark grass in the foreground; the paler grass in the middle ground; the dark green shrubs in the middle distance; the band of yellow-green fields still further into the distance; the blue distant hills. Vertical trees overlap these five bands, linking them and the sky above.

**Defining depth:** By placing similarly shaped trees in both foreground and middle ground, and by placing a seated woman in the foreground and a standing woman in the middle ground, Monet conveys a clear sense of depth. You can do the same in a garden with objects of known size: a bench, fence railing, planted pots, or chairs.

**Scale:** When we have something of known size in a garden, we better understand the size of objects around that object. Monet uses the two human figures and an umbrella to clarify scale as well as distance.

**Movement:** The far-right tree in this painting and the tall one to its left best define the movement of the wind just as willow trees, ornamental grasses, and other wispy plants do in your garden.

**Color harmony:** Pastel greens and blues establish the softness of the light and the scene. Using this color palette in your garden creates a feeling of calm.

Figure 5.1A: Three trees in the author's meadow, photograph by the author. We often retreat to the simple contemplative beauty of the bench under these oaks in our meadow under billowing clouds.

## Garden

**Tall trees in a flat meadow:** We planted three pin oaks (*Quercus palustris*) in our meadow, about a hundred feet from the main garden, to create a shaded, gently enclosed place to sit in our often sunny Vermont meadow. Trees make this a place for people. On a spring day, with eighteen acres of dandelions in bloom, this is a tranquil space to sit. From a distance, the vertical trees contrast with the horizontal field to draw visitors to them.

**Sense of enclosure:** We wanted to be able to sit in the meadow, one of the most beautiful places on our property, but simply placing a bench out there did not give it a sense of place. We planted the three oaks and then, with my riding lawn mower, I mowed a circle of lawn

around the oaks weekly as well as a path that runs from the garden proper out to that circle of lawn under the three oaks. We set the bench to encourage people to look out at the meadow, not back at the garden. Place your benches with an eye to what people sitting on that bench will see when they look straight ahead.

**Color harmony:** In the spring, this sitting area is a study in acid yellow of dandelions and many greens. At other times of the year the colors change dramatically to enliven this space, just as the colors in your garden, fields, and meadows change. Notice those changes. Garden writer Mac Griswold said, "Gardening is the slowest of the performing arts."

Figure 5.2: Didier Nolet, Chicago-based contemporary artist, *Snapping Trail* (inspired by a trail in the Warren Dunes State Park in Michigan), 2004, by and used with permission of the artist. Light is the source of life. Pay attention to it. Plant to define it. Nolet paints light first, trees second.

## Painting

**Defining depth:** First, Nolet establishes the foundation of the painting: the bronze-beige meadow grasses that run in a band across the bottom. Next, he establishes two large arcing dark green trees to the right and left; he links these two at ground level with dark green grass. He uses the two masses of darker trees to frame the lighter trees in the background, thereby establishing depth. The decreasing sharpness of foliage from front to back also establishes depth, due in part to the fact that humidity in the air filters light and turns it bluish, thereby blurring the edges of distant objects.

**Architectural balance:** The painting is divided into five areas: the grassy base; the two dark green masses of trees to the right and left; the light green center; the white sky above. You could model a tree planting on this painting: two separate blocks of dark-green-leaved trees in the foreground with a gathering of chartreuse-leaved trees in the gap behind.

**Itinerary of the eye:** *The way in:* the light-colored space between the large trees to the right and left leads your eye into the painting. The lightness, especially to the right, implies there is an open meadow between foreground and background trees. *The way out:* the pink light to the far left of the painting as well as the pink light at the base and tops of the far-left trees are places for the eye to escape. Across the top, Nolet releases the painting into the atmosphere.

**Unity through color:** The artist suffuses everything with greens; herein is the central theme and variation of this painting. He then repeats the warm pink-orange highlights of the grasses in some of the leaves in the foreground trees to link them visually.

**Light:** Above all, this is a painting about light. As Nolet told me, "We are drawn to light. Our memories are triggered by it, informed by it."

Figure 5.2A: A garden in the Berkshire Hills of Massachusetts, photograph by Margaret Hensel, used with permission from Positive Images. Light differs from one part of the country to the next, in large part due to levels of humidity (or lack thereof). Here, humidity and shade from trees softens light.

## Garden

**Defining depth:** The garden itself is a series of layers: green grass, yellow coreopsis, mixed annuals and perennials, white cosmos, and white fence. The house and trees form the middle ground and between those trees we see the distant ridgeline in the bluish gray created by humidity. (This blue-gray atmosphere is seen only in humid parts of the country; in the southwest, for example, sunlight passes through dry air and so the light is bright and washes out subtler colors.)

**Architectural balance:** The fence is the horizontal line running through this garden image; it is a built structure that anchors the garden and ties it through color and material to the house. The columns echo the formality of the architecture.

**Unity through color:** As in the base of Nolet's painting, the yellow coreopsis runs along the entire foreground to form the base for the garden. Variety lies in annuals and perennials in the middle ground. White cosmos then runs the full length of the upper level of the bed and repeats the white of the fence and house. White echoes appear in the pink-white cleome and shasta daisies. Zinnias, echinops, and, later in the season, *Sedum spectabile* provide color accents in this elegant border.

Figure 5.3: Charles-François Daubigny (1817–1863), *Landscape,* 1863, in the collection of and used with permission from the Sterling and Francine Clark Art Institute, Williamstown, Massachusetts. Trees enclose this pond; they give it a space, a context. Trees make places, and small- to medium-size trees make places of human scale.

# CREATING INTIMACY

## Painting

**Light:** Daubigny, a precursor to the impressionists, is interested in the play of light on the trees, water, and the hazy distant hillside. The dark vertical tree trunks make light feel bright through contrast.

**Itinerary of the eye:** The lower-left corner of this painting, as in Lucien Abrams' (figure 5.5), is dark, as is the lower right. These two dark passages contrast with and frame the lighter pond, a light shape that carries your eye back to the rowboat. Your eye then slips up the light green bank to the opening in the pollarded trees and then on up to the sky. The outer branches on the far-right trees lead your eye across the sky at the top of the painting, then your eye slides down the far-left panel of sky to begin the journey again at the bottom of the canvas.

**Composition:** Trees tie all parts together by their mass and line. Daubigny repeats the thick trunks and wispy tops of the pollarded willows as a line that runs horizontally across the lower middle of the painting. The reflection of four of these trees in the strong S-shape body of water ties the middle of the painting to the foreground. The mass of trees to the right holds your eye in the painting. Light filters throughout.

**Color:** This painting echoes the tonalist school wherein painters captured the tone or feeling of a scene, in large part with muted browns, greens, and bronzes. Your garden in autumn could be a tonalist painting.

Figure 5.3A: Mount Cuba Gardens, Greenville, Delaware, photograph by the author. Use trees to define the edges of spaces, to enclose areas. The surface of a pond doubles the number of trees in this contemplative garden.

## Garden

**Reflected light:** Like Daubigny, the designers of this park made sure that visitors would be able to walk around the pond, thereby enabling people to see the reflection of the trees on the pond's surface from every side. Chairs on both sides of the pond underpin this intention. If you have a pond, plant trees around it to take advantage of the reflective nature of water and then set benches to show your best view.

**Visual unity:** The reflection of the trees and sky on the surface of the water doubles the intention of the designers and further celebrates the native landscape and flora of the Delaware Piedmont.

**Framed views:** The thoughtful pruning of the trees and the mowing of the central lawn path allow your eye to carry you across this pond and into the distant meadow.

**Color and light contrast:** The feeling of being within a green shady copse of trees near a pond is heightened by the contrasting view to the sunny meadow of blonde grasses and specimen trees just moving into their colorful fall foliage. Daubigny noticed this source of beauty too.

**Man-made and natural objects gently contrast:** The gray teak chairs and the gray rowboat provide a gentle note of contrast with this otherwise green natural setting. Both chairs and boat offer access and respite as well as establish scale.

Figure 5.4: William Chadwick (1879– 1962), *March Snow,* in the collection of and used with permission from the Florence Griswold Museum, Old Lyme, Connecticut. In winter, when trees have lost their leaves, the darkness of their trunks and the silhouette of their branching becomes a compelling element of a garden.

## TREES IN WINTER

### Painting

**Seeing beauty in a spare landscape:** It takes artists to see and then paint images that we might pass by. Here, Chadwick shows us the restrained beauty of a winter scene, an image that might show you a new way to look at the woodland around your home in winter.

**Composition:** The ascending black trunks and branches of the trees contrast to the mounding white snow and the horizon in the background. Through this vertical/horizontal scene runs the reverse S-curve

of the stream. The right-leaning branches of the trees move the image as does the flow of the snow down from the far left and then up toward the far right. The beige saplings in the lower left of the painting reinforce this left-to-right movement.

**Unity:** Color supports the unity provided by strong composition. By limiting the colors to blacks and grays, white and beige, and its related pale yellow, the image holds together.

Figure 5.4A: Snow-covered tree trunks, photograph by Jerry Howard. Like Chadwick, Howard sees the beauty of white snow as it has been driven into the textured bark of this grove of dark-trunked trees.

## Garden

**Black trunks in a white landscape:** These closely growing tree trunks etched white with snow lie in stark contrast to the line of evergreen trees in the background. Wanting to emphasize their verticality, the owner pruned the lower branches off. You could do the same with virtually any grove of trees or mixed woodland.

**Animation:** When you walk by these trunks at any time of the year, but especially in winter, they align and realign constantly as you move past them or among them. The result is movement within a static scene: your movement creates the action among realigning trunks.

**Composition:** It's very simple in the winter garden: vertical brown-black lines on a horizontal white landscape. The starkness is powerful in its simplicity. We just need to take the time to see that beauty.

Figure 5.5: Lucien Abrams (1870–1941), *The Orchard*, 1916, in the collection of and used with permission from the Florence Griswold Museum, Old Lyme, Connecticut. Planting even a small orchard will give you so much pleasure, lots of fruit, and create a satisfying grid of trees to walk within.

# THE ORCHARD AND ALLÉE: LINES OF TREES AS STRUCTURAL ELEMENTS

## Painting

**The beauty of a functioning orchard:** Abrams and other American impressionists rented rooms at Florence Griswold's home in Old Lyme, Connecticut, starting in the early 1890s. This painting is of the old apple orchard between her house and the Lieutenant River, which you can just make out under the far trees. Part of the beauty comes from the functioning geometry of a working orchard.

**The same tree repeated many times in the landscape to define depth:** Abrams chose to set up his easel very close to the first tree so as to clarify the distance between trees in this orchard. These fruit trees have been pruned to show the architecture of trunk and branches. The interest for the painter is complexity within simplicity.

**Itinerary of the eye:** Abrams adds visual weight to the lower-left corner of his painting by placing the shadow of the closest tree, with its largest, darkest trunk, so as to anchor that corner of the painting. Your eye then goes to the woman sitting near the lower-right corner and then it slides deep into the picture to be captured by the light horizontal line of the distant river.

**Impressionism and light:** As with the impressionists working in France, Abrams is interested in the exploding dots of light reflecting off the apple blossoms and even patches of branches. Pools of light shimmer on the meadow grass while dark blue pools of shadow gather under each tree. Dark red outlines on some of the upper branches contrast with emerging foliage, unifying the painting.

**Framing:** The trunks and branches of the trees frame any number of views into other parts of the orchard and toward the river.

Figure 5.5A: The author's crab apple orchard in his Vermont garden, photograph by Richard Brown. I prune only interior twigs and branches of crab apples to show their sculptural trunking; I never prune exterior branches. Let a tree be.

## Garden

**The orchard provides structure in a garden:** I remember the arresting beauty of lines of Macintosh and Cortland apple trees in bloom every spring on the orchard I grew up on in Connecticut. When Mary and I began developing our garden, we quoted the orchard with three rows of flowering crab apples.

**Itinerary:** We want to walk through the orchard, where rows of trees and their overarching branches frame views to the right and left of the central path. We set the sculpture on a pedestal as a focal point (like Abrams' woman under the tree) within the brick path to draw people into the next garden area.

**Impressionism in the garden:** Look at this photograph with squinted eyes and you'll see the same exploding dots of color in the apple blossoms that Abrams captured in his painting. The large Macintosh apple tree in the background as well as the crab apples provide an impressionist look in the spring. In winter, their persistent fruits are red or yellow dots against white snow and blue sky.

**Shadow:** The dark green of the two yew sentinels on either side of the entry into the garden has the same visual weight as the dark green shadows under the apple trees in Abrams' painting. They stand in pleasing contrast to the shimmer of light in the trees.

Figure 5.6 Gustav Klimt (1862–1918), *The Park*, 1910, in the collection of the Museum of Modern Art, New York, New York, photograph © 2008 MOMA, licensed by SCALA/Art Resource, New York, New York. Artists teach us to see the branching and foliage of trees in new ways. Cover the lower sixth of this painting with your finger and watch leaves become nonrepresentational and abstract. Now go outside and look at your trees in a new way.

# LOW-PRUNED TREES COMPRESS VIEWS UNDER THEM

## Painting

**Foliage:** Klimt's *The Park* shows how light bounces off foliage to erase all individual leaves, thereby creating an abstract shimmer. (Contrast this treatment of leaves with John Lee Fitch's in figure 4.2.) This painting helps you see foliage on trees in a new way. In fact, helping us see in new ways is one of the key roles of art. As Maya Lin, architect and creator of the Vietnam Veteran's Memorial wall, said, "Art is the act of an individual willing to say something new, something not quite familiar." To put it another way, Sir George Sitwell wrote in 1909: "In every garden there should be some element of wonder or surprise, if only to make recollection more vivid."

**Light and dark:** The weight and mass of the upper foliage compresses the light in the lower left, where the lower branches of the trees are high enough to allow light to come through. The vertical trunks of these low-pruned trees punctuate the light with dark verticals. The even-darker-green hedge in the lower-right corner creates another level of contrast with the highly confined light area in the lower-left corner.

**Focal point:** By virtue of her dark full-length dress, the female figure is almost indistinguishable from the foliage. She remains, however, a focal point. Without the white decorative circles on her dress, she would appear treelike and fuse with the background.

**Depth:** Klimt gives only the slightest hints as to the depth of this scene in a public park. Clearly hundreds of feet of distance exist between foreground and background, yet the painter has used color and the mass of upper foliage to flatten depth.

Figure 5.6A: A Patrick Chasse design for a garden on an island off the coast of Maine, photograph by the author. Pruning or not pruning the lower branches of trees can help you create a multitude of effects: lowering or towering canopies; leafy scrims you have to brush out of the way; entrances; barriers; compressed views under them.

## Garden

**Compressing a view:** When landscape architect Patrick Chasse directed the pruning of dead branches in this woodland, he wanted to compress views from the woods out to the water. The result is a greater feeling of being *within* the spruce forest.

**Vertical/horizontal:** By emphasizing the horizontality of the blue band of water, the verticality of the dark gray spruce trunks is made even more emphatic. As you walk over the bridge and along the horizontal surface of the earth toward the shore, the verticality of the trees becomes especially apparent. Each pair of tree trunks frames yet another view to the blue water and sky, just as they do in the Klimt painting.

**Focal point:** The slightly arching man-made bridge provides a visual anchor and counterpoint to the natural landscape.

**Pleasing contrast:** The contrast between the geometric man-made bridge and the natural forms of the spruce trees, the shoreline, and water set up a pleasing contrast that gives this image its clarity. (See also figure 4.7.)

**Color and unity:** Chasse had the bridge built of unpainted cedar so that its gray color would eventually echo that of the silver gray of the lichen on the spruce trunks as well as gray granite bedrock and the sometimes gray water. These trees become sculptures; Klimt's trees become mass.

Figure 5.7: Vincent van Gogh, *Road Workers in Saint Remy,* 1889, in the Phillips Collection, Washington, D.C.; photo by Erich Lessing, Art Resource, New York, New York. As van Gogh shows you, the trunks of trees and their major lower branches frame views between them. Prune lower branches thoughtfully to define the edges of those views.

# POSITIVE AND NEGATIVE SPACE

## Painting

**Trunks and branches shape views:** In this striking, diagonally composed painting, van Gogh's primary subject is the row of four trees, their trunks outlined in black to emphasize their shapes. The views between those trunks are also of great interest to him. The scene between the left side of the canvas and the first tree is a balanced painting in itself. He gathered the darkest darks and the lightest lights in this corner: the women's black dresses with white collars; the black door with its white trim; the green shutters and orange wall. The apparently negative space between that first trunk and the edge of the painting is a compelling vignette. The space between the next two trunks is also a little painting focused on the green door and the two road workers, yet it is clearly subordinate to the first. The spaces between trees two and three and three and four are of diminishing size, clarity, and interest, but

the artist introduces the only red in the painting into those negative spaces to draw your eye deep into the painting. He reinforces that by painting the last tree trunk a deep green to hold your eye in the canvas.

**Branches frame shapes high in the trees:** The black-outlined branches in the trees also create shapes between them. Look only at the spaces between the branches and you will see such sweeps and curls and activity in orange heightened by the blue sky and orange foliage. Too often, when looking at trees, we see only the positive space—the tree trunk, branches, and foliage. Pay attention to the space between those branches, and you'll gain a whole new level of appreciation not only about trees but also about how all trees and shrubs frame views between their branching.

Figure 5.7A: An oak tree in a park in Marblehead, Massachusetts, photograph by the author. Because tree trunks and their branches frame views, don't be afraid to plant trees between your house and a fine view. Trees enliven views by introducing variety.

## Garden

**Trunk and branches frame views:** Because the trunk of this oak tree is so dark, it stands out in contrast to the sun-lit sea, sky, and distant spits of land. The branches and trunk are the positive space. But if we look at the spaces they shape, you'll see that just as van Gogh is showing us, the branches and trunk frame views. Notice how the trunk and the far left of the photograph frame a view of a distant spit of land as well as sea and sky. Notice that the two main branches coming off the right side of the tree shape a segment of the sky and how the lower-right branches and leaves, in concert with the land and the fence, frame a view of the distant promontory and sailboats going into the harbor.

**Assess your own trees:** Every single tree in your garden is framing views right now. Some are harmonious—that is, negative and positive space are in harmony and balance. Others might be less so, but pruning may be able to create even clearer, more interesting frames. You might want to go out there right now to see.

"*Color in a picture is like enthusiasm in life.*"

—Vincent van Gogh

# COLOR HARMONY OR CONTRAST

Throughout this book, I've been looking at many design elements—line, form or shape, mass, unity—that go into composing and developing paintings and garden designs. Getting colors right in a painting is complex; getting them right in the garden is, in a sense, even more complex. Unlike a painting, a garden exists in time. Colors constantly shift with the changing light of day, with the changing color of flowers as the days or weeks go by, and as the initial color of flowers fade. There is no point in being discouraged by this complexity. As photographer and garden writer Richard Hartlage said in his book *Bold Visions for the Garden:* "It is a color glutton's paradise out there, so have fun."

At the same time, it's important to know some of the basics of color so that you can have fun with reds, yellows, blues, oranges, purples, and all the other colors in your garden. To the eyes of many, when we look at a garden or a painting, our eyes are drawn to color first. Garden writer Stephen Lacey wrote, "The eye appreciates colour before it appreciates shape." Paul Gauguin, the French painter, concurs: "Colors, although less numerous than lines, are still more explicative by virtue of their potent influence on the eye." Take another look at figure 4.6 and you'll see that your eye goes to red before line. Our eye does go first to color, then on to line and form, yet in the end, all three need to integrate to form a beautiful whole. Knitting together form and color into a coordinated harmony is the essence of art.

Color is made all the more interesting by the fact that one color affects adjacent ones to set up vibrancy. Place red tulips in a groundcover of blue scilla and you create one look, but place the acid green of *Euphorbia polychroma* in their midst and everything changes.

To give you a practical grounding in color, I asked my friend Sydney Eddison to explore color in the garden by describing her recently published *The Gardener's Color Wheel.* If you want to learn more about her take on color in the garden, read her book *The Gardener's Palette: Creating Color in the Garden.* Both are practical and approachable.

Figures 6.1 and 6.2: *The Gardener's Color Wheel*, used with permission by Sydney Eddison, creator, and Ken Haines, owner of The Color Wheel Company, Philomath, Oregon (www.thegardenerscolor wheel.com). Deciding on color combinations in your garden can be daunting. Learning to use this color wheel will add immeasurably to your confidence as you make color choices in your garden.

# THE GARDENER'S COLOR WHEEL    *By Sydney Eddison*

*The Gardener's Color Wheel* is a low-tech guide to using color in the garden. It is based on the original color wheel published in 1766 by British engraver Moses Harris in a slim volume called *The Natural System of Colours.*

Harris based his system on the order of the colors in the rainbow—red, orange, yellow, green, blue, and violet—because ". . . if red and yellow be mixed together they will compose orange." He observed in the arrangement of colors a natural progression from red to red-orange to orange to yellow-orange to yellow and so forth, which suggested to him the circular diagram. Thus, he placed orange between its parents, red and yellow. Green obviously belonged between yellow and blue, and violet between blue and red.

This arrangement clearly shows the "harmonious connections" between adjacent hues, which share a common pigment. To Harris, all the orange hues were harmonious. Lying between red and yellow and containing pigment from both parents, they were members of the same color family and therefore, like each other. Harmony is based on likeness. In the garden and elsewhere, the effect of harmony is serene and restful. But too much harmony can be boring.

Contrast, which is based on difference, produces the opposite effect. It can be startling, exciting, and sometimes jarring. Harris made note that the extreme contrast between colors that lie directly opposite each other on the color wheel, such as red and green, yellow

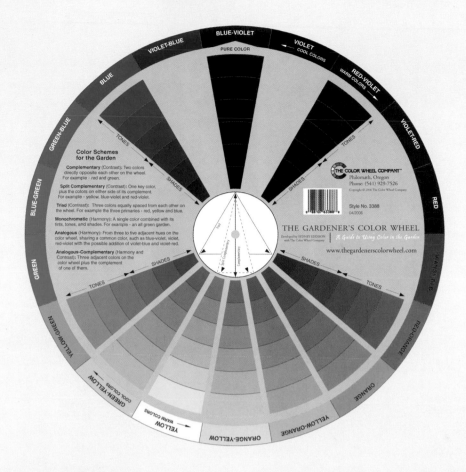

and violet, blue and orange, create a bold eye-catching effect. Placed side by side, these so-called complementary colors always command attention.

Contrast and harmony are the building blocks in every art form. There really isn't any other way to use color. And a color wheel shows you which colors are alike and therefore harmonious and which colors are different from one another and so, contrasting.

Although there are many more hues in the natural and man-made worlds than would fit on any color wheel, they all belong somewhere in this continuum of related hues. It is up to the artist or gardener to study the colors carefully and to understand where they belong.

Approximately where does the delicate green of early spring foliage fit into the color picture? It is certainly not the same color as midsummer foliage. The spring green has more yellow in it; therefore, it belongs on the yellow side of green. You may not find the exact color on the color wheel, but you now know where it would belong.

While artists have to mix their own hues, nature has provided gardeners with an infinite range of pure colors, lighter tints, and deeper tones and shades. Thus, The Gardener's Color Wheel offers an expanded range of hues. Progressively lighter tints appear in concentric rings on one side of the wheel, the deeper tones and shades on the other.

## How to Use the Gardener's Color Wheel
*By Sydney Eddison*

1. **Look across your garden:** First, look carefully at the colors in your garden, using the wheel as a reference. Figure out roughly where some of the foliage and flower colors in your garden come closest to matching those on the wheel.

2. **To create contrast:** Choose one favorite color in your garden and match it to the color closest to it on the wheel. Now, turn the pointer to it. For a lively contrast, consult the diagram arrow in the middle of the wheel. It will show you the complementary color from the opposite side of the wheel.

   If your color of choice was a yellow hue, for example, you will find a violet hue in the opening opposite. In the garden, purple violets would make a charming contrast to yellow primroses in the spring. A summer contrast might involve orange daylilies with blue globe thistles. And red winterberries always look especially brilliant against any evergreen foliage in the winter.

3. **To create harmony:** To create pleasing harmony, stick to colors that are next to each other on the color wheel. While there are seven adjacent openings on the Gardener's Color Wheel, limit your choice to three or four colors, such as violet, blue violet, and red violet. Likeness results in harmony. Reds containing blue can also be used successfully with members of the violet family.

   But red is a difficult color in the garden, and also in printer's ink. Suffice it to say that red containing blue and red containing orange are very different from each other and are therefore rarely harmonious. While you may not find the red you have in the garden on the color wheel, you can consult the wheel to determine whether it is a cool red containing blue or a warm red containing orange.

4. **Making comparisons:** Making comparisons is what it is all about, and using a color wheel for reference sharpens your eye and increases the accuracy of your perception.

✧ ✧ ✧ ✧

With your new understanding of color, you might want to go into your garden and do what Vita Sackville-West did in hers to develop new color combinations. She snipped a flower stem at ground level and tied that stem to a slim bamboo stake, leaving six to eight inches of the bamboo free of the stem at the bottom. She then walked throughout her garden, pushing that stake into the ground next to other blooming perennials to see how their colors reacted to one another. Once she discovered a satisfying new combination that worked for both flower as well as foliage color and shape, she recorded it in her garden diary. When autumn came, she would transplant one next to the other to create a new color combination.

Now let's examine various ways to look at color in the garden. Then I'll close this chapter with a pairing of paintings and gardens to further explore how painters and garden designers have used color in similar ways.

## COLOR SCHEMES FOR THE GARDEN

**Complementary (contrast):** Two colors directly opposite each other on the wheel (red and green, yellow and violet, blue and orange). Dramatic contrasts result.

**Split complementary (contrast):** One key color, plus the colors on either side of its complement. For example, yellow, blue violet, and red violet.

**Triad (contrast):** Three colors equally spaced from each other on the wheel. For example, the three primaries—red, yellow, blue.

**Monochromatic (harmony):** A single color combined with its tints, tones, and shades. For example, an all-green garden.

**Analagous complementary (harmony and contrast):** Three adjacent colors on the wheel plus the complement of one of them.

**Pure color:** Any hue at full intensity; the pure colors are on the outermost ring of the color wheel.

**Color temperature:** This describes the emotional impact of color.

## THE VOCABULARY OF COLOR

**Warm colors:** Reds, oranges, and yellows; they produce heat and excitement because they recall red-hot embers, flames, and the summer sun. Warm colors advance toward the viewer.

**Cool colors:** Greens, blues, violets; they produce emotions and memories of cool ocean waves, restful green depths of a forest, and the bracing chill of purple mountaintops. Cool colors recede from the viewer.

**Primary colors:** Red, yellow, and blue are primary colors, and all other colors are made from these three.

**Secondary colors:** Orange, green, and violet are formed by mixing two primary colors. Orange is composed of red and yellow; green is composed of yellow and blue; violet is composed of blue and red.

**In-between colors:** All in-between colors are made from different proportions of one primary and one secondary color. For example, violet blue contains both primary blue and secondary violet.

**Hue:** Another name for color.

**Tint:** Any color plus white.

**Tone:** Any color plus gray.

**Shade:** Any color plus black.

**Value:** The qualities of lightness or darkness in colors are called values, but you can also talk about light colors and dark colors. Yellow is the lightest, violet is the darkest. All you have to do is squint at the color wheel to see this for yourself.

## THE POWER OF WHITE

Technically speaking, white is not a color at all. But in the garden it is a force to be reckoned with. White is lighter, brighter, and more riveting than any color in the rainbow. One white blossom in a colorful flower garden will draw the eye like a magnet and steal the show. So use it wisely. Contrary to conventional wisdom, white does not provide unity between clashing colors. Gray is much better at that job.

## GREEN: KEEPER OF THE PEACE

Green is the great peacekeeper. It is nature's choice as a background color whenever there is enough rainfall. In the natural landscape, colors don't clash because they are woven together by this cool undemanding hue. Green does not call attention to itself, like the bright colors and white, nor does it vanish into the distance, like the dark blues and violets. Even the most incompatible color schemes can be harmonized by the soothing presence of green.

## GRAYS AND GRAY GREENS

Favor low-intensity tints, tones, and shades of gray or gray green to tie a garden together.

Here's a story about gray: garden designer MaryAnne McGourty once got a call from a client who said she was having a wedding in five days. Could MaryAnne come along to improve her flower border for the event? She gathered up a number of pots in her nursery that held gray-leaved plants, removed redundant plants in her client's garden, and replaced them with gray-leaved perennials. The whole border came together in a very new and handsome way. (See Karen Bussolini's book, *Elegant Silvers.*)

## CONTRASTING COLORS IN THE GARDEN

### Blue and Orange
- Blue agapanthus flowers next to the orange *Crocosmia* 'Lucifer'
- Blue *Lobelia siphilitica* and an orange monarch butterfly
- The blue sky and orange fall foliage
- A blue bench next to orange *Geum coccineum* 'Borisii'
- *Aconitum carmichaelii* 'Barker's Variety' and *Helenium autumnale* 'Moerheim Beauty'
- The annual blue torenia with *Impatiens* 'Tango' in a pot
- *Salvia* 'Indigo Spires' and *Lilium* 'Enchantment'
- *Aconitum carmichaelii* with *Campsis radicans* (orange-flowering trumpet vine)

### Yellow and Violet
- Yellow tulips with *Ajuga reptans* 'Atropurpurea'
- *Iris pallida* 'Variegata' with *Anemone blanda*
- *Primula veris* with violets
- *Allium aflatunense* with laburnum flowers
- *Alchemilla mollis* and *Salvia verticillata* 'Purple Rain'
- *Rudbeckia hirta* 'Irish Eyes' with *Clematis* x *jackmanii*
- *Forsythia* 'Meadowlark' underplanted with *Tulipa* 'Queen of the Night'

### Red and Green
- Red leaves in the fall on a green lawn
- *Dahlia* 'Red Riding Hood' next to a boxwood hedge
- Any red flower and its plant's own green foliage
- Red maple against green mountain and blue sky

*To create pleasing harmony, stick to colors that are next to each other on the color wheel. Limit your choice to three or four colors, such as violet, blue violet and red violet. Likeness results in harmony.*

## HARMONIOUS COLORS IN THE GARDEN

### Spring
- Hellebores, *Brunnera macrophylla* 'Jack Frost' (blue flower, white variegated leaf), crocuses, *Pulmonaria* 'Mawson's Blue'
- *Iberis sempervirens* (white), *Lathyrus vernus* (purple, blue red), and *Brunnera macrophylla* 'Jack Frost' (forget-me-not blue)
- *Dicentra spectabilis* 'Alba' (white bleedingheart) and *Veronica gentianoides* (soft blue)

### Early Summer
- *Rosa glauca* (light pink), *Papaver orientale* 'Helen Elizabeth' (pink), and *Artemisia alba* 'Canescens' (gray foliage)
- *Persicaria bistorta* 'Superba' (light pink), *Viburnum plicatum* 'Shasta' (white), and *Paeonia* 'Claudia' (bright reddish pink)
- *Stachys macrantha* 'Superba' (deep pink), *Alchemilla mollis* (chartreuse), and *Oenothera stricta* 'Sulphurea' (pink stems, pale yellow flowers)

### High Summer
- *Delphinium grandiflorum* 'Blue Butterfly' and *Sidalcea* 'Elsie Heugh' (a soft pink)
- *Helictotrichon sempervirens* 'Sapphire' (blue oat grass) with *Allium christophii* (purple).
- *Alchemilla mollis* (chartreuse), *Salvia verticillata* 'Purple Rain', and *Veronica spicata* 'Red Fox'

### Late Summer
- *Coreopsis verticillata* 'Moonbeam' (pastel yellow), *Crocosmia* x *crocosmiiflora* 'Solfaterre' (yellow/bronze) and *Salvia nemorosa* 'Lubeca' (violet)
- *Anemone vitifolia* 'Robustissima' (soft pink), *Galtonia candicans* (a white-flowering bulb), and *Nicotiana sylvestris* (white, an annual)
- *Cimicifuga ramosa* 'Hillside Black Beauty' (white flowers, burgundy leaves), *Eupatorium maculatum* 'Gateway' (soft pink), and *Panicum virgatum* 'Shenandoah' (with burgundy hints in foliage)

# COLOR COMBINATIONS
## Chartreuse, Orange, White, and Yellow with Shadows for Black

Figure 6.3: Pierre Bonnard (1867– 1947), *Autumn, the Grape Harvest*, 1912, in the collection of the Pushkin Museum of Fine Arts, Moscow, Russia, photo credit SCALA/Art Resource, New York, New York, © 2008 The Artists Rights Society, New York/ADAGP, Paris, France. Contrasting chartreuse with orange and black causes the chartreuse to pop. Take advantage of chartreuse-leaved coleus, for example, to lighten up a dark corner, or use chartreuse and dark foliage plants as a theme for a dramatic garden.

Figure 6.3A: The *Robinia pseudoacacia* 'Frisia' in the author's garden in the North Cotswold Hills of England, photograph by Andrew Lawson. The sunny chartreuse leaves of this tree on the shady north side of our cottage gives the impression the sun is shining on our garden all day long.

Figure 6.4: Raoul Dufy (1877–1953), *The Harvest*, 1929, in the collection of the Tate Gallery, London, England, photo credit Tate Gallery/Art Resource, New York, New York. Dufy placed complementary colors, those opposite or nearly opposite one another on the color wheel, next to one another to create the shimmer and vibrations of this autumn scene. He placed red next to green, blue or dark green next to orange. He also placed analogous colors next to one another for harmony, as in the upper field where yellow and orange harmonize.

Figure 6.4A: The author's garden in Vermont in October, photograph by the author. Nature, with a little help from gardeners, creates this same shimmer in our Vermont garden (and across the northeast) every October. This look is all based on juxtaposing colors opposite one another on the color wheel: orange leaves on a green lawn with blue sky above.

Figure 6.5: Paul Gauguin (1848–1903), *Women and a White Horse*, 1903, in the collection of and used with permission from the Museum of Fine Arts, Boston, Massachusetts. This warm combination of yellows, reds, oranges, and pinks predominates. Gauguin heightens these warm colors by contrasting them with cooler greens, violets, and blues, thereby capturing the heat of the South Pacific Islands.

Figure 6.5A: Powys Castle Garden, Wales, United Kingdom, photograph by the author. The garden designers here chose similar warm colors in the long-blooming alstromerias, along with other flowering perennials. The green foliage as well as soft green meadows in the backdrop provide cooler contrasting colors.

Figure 6.6: Henri Matisse (1869–1954), *Gate of the Casbah*, 1912–1913, in the collection of the Pushkin Museum of Fine Arts, Moscow, Russia, photo credit SCALA/Art Resource, New York, New York, © 2008 Artists Rights Society, New York/ADAGP, Paris, France. Red and blue are nearly opposite one another on the color wheel; gray and blue gray bring these contrasting colors closer together, just as gray will do in your garden.

Figure 6.6A: Karen Bussolini's garden in northwestern Connecticut, photograph by Karen Bussolini. Bussolini uses contrasting colors—red and blue, for example—to bring drama to her garden and then uses gray-leaved plants to bring a degree of harmony between opposites. This can be seen in the combination of *Stachys byzantina* 'Helene Von Stein', *Nepeta* 'Six Hills Giant', *Salvia* 'May Night', *Veronica* 'Crater Lake Blue', *Papaver* 'Turkenlouis', and *Rosa* 'Robusta'.

Figure 6.7: Amedeo Bocchi (1883–1976), *In the Park,* in the collection of the Galleria Communale d'Arte Moderna, Rome, Italy, photo credit SCALA/Art Resource, New York, New York. The yellow orange of the woman's blouse is opposite the color wheel from her purple-black dress, hat, and shoes. This arresting portrait gains force through these complementary colors. Yellow highlights on the lawn contrast with the black-green woods in the background. In the foreground, dots of red and pink flowers in the contrasting green lawn as well as red in the pillow, the underside of her hat, and her lips provide gentle highlights.

Figure 6.7A: The Bellevue Botanical Gardens, Bellevue, Washington: *Geum coccineum* 'Fire Lake' and *Heuchera americana* 'Palace Passion', with daylily foliage, photograph by Robin Cushman. You can translate the Bocchi painting (figure 6.7) into your garden by using some of the same color combinations used in this garden in the Pacific Northwest.

Figure 6.8: Henri Matisse (1869–1954), *The Bedroom (Le Boudoir)*, 1921, in the collection of the Musée de l'Orangerie, Paris, France, © 2008 Artists Rights Society, New York/ADAGP, Paris, France. The languorous feeling in this painting emanates as much from the soft pastel gray, blue, and pink tones as from the subject matter of two women lazing in a boudoir. (A tone is a color muted by the addition of gray.) Only two red flowers in a vase and reflected in the mirror offer contrasting highlights.

Figure 6.8A: Artist Thyrza Whittemore's garden, photograph by Karen Bussolini. Because you have available all the pastels Matisse uses in his painting as well as many others, you can translate color combinations in your favorite paintings into your garden. Here is a variation on Matisse's theme in Thyrza Whittemore's garden.

Figure 6.9: Hugo Grenville, contemporary British artist, *Still Life with Poppies, Orchid and Dutch Coffee Pot,* 2006, courtesy of the painter and the Wally Findlay Galleries, New York, New York, and Palm Beach, Florida. Whereas Matisse in *The Bedroom (Le Boudoir)* chose colors within a very limited range of pastels, Grenville opens up the color range, as you could, to include pastel greens, yellows, and oranges with red highlights. Note also that Grenville juxtaposes colors opposite the color wheel—soft greens and reds, soft oranges and blues—to bring vitality to his painting.

Figure 6.9A: The Northwest Garden Nursery, Eugene, Oregon—allium, kniphofia, sedum, crocosmia, dahlia, lily, and black mondo grass, photograph by Robin Cushman. You could use this color combination, or this actual plant combination, to introduce subtle color interplay in one of your borders.

*"My garden is my most beautiful masterpiece."*

—Claude Monet (1840–1926)

# BRINGING IT ALL TOGETHER: CLAUDE MONET'S LIFE, GARDEN, AND ART

*I*n Claude Monet's life, painting and gardening were utterly interwoven as with none other. To get to the heart of his life and work, however, we must fight our way back—as you'll see artist Leslie Parke does in her essay below—through the commercialization of the man and his work. We have to rid our minds of decades of coffee mugs, note cards, and cheap posters of his water lily paintings. We have to sort our way through an avalanche of postcards and calendars, tea towels, and trinkets to get to the original work of this man and artist who changed so very much about how we see not only paintings but also gardens.

Monet was born in Paris on November 14, 1840. When he was five, the family moved to Le Havre, Normandy. There his father, as well as an aunt, tended ornamental gardens; as a boy and young student of art, Monet drew and sketched in those gardens as well as drawing caricatures of local people.

Father wanted son to follow in his footsteps in the grocery store business, but Monet's interest in art was already apparent. In 1851, at age eleven, he went to the secondary school for the arts in Le Havre. By age sixteen, he had met marine artist Eugène Boudin, who had a shop close to his home. Boudin became his mentor and taught him to paint outdoors—*en plein aire*. In 1857, his mother died; he left school and went to live with his aunt, a gardener. In 1861, he went into military service in Algiers but returned home, having contracted typhoid. He regained his health and began to study art in Paris, where he met Pierre-Auguste Renoir, Frederic Bazille, and Alfred Sisley. Together, they and others founded what became impressionism.

Change within the city of Paris, as well as the world of art, was all around Monet. Napoleon III was transforming a filthy city; great public parks and gardens were created, whereas before gardens were typically limited to enclosed gardens near schools in Paris. The Industrial Revolution was in full swing and, with it, an emerging middle class. With money to spend, middle-class French began to plant gardens around their homes and buy paintings to put in them; an interest in horticulture was expanding in France, Holland, and, especially, England, a country Monet visited first in 1870 and later in 1900.

This second visit was at a time when the great English garden designer Gertrude Jekyll (1843–1942) was maturing her work in Surrey, just south of London, and formulating her color theories for the garden, theories that she published in 1908 in her influential book *Colour Schemes for the Flower Garden*. Monet subscribed to gardening journals and received plant catalogues. No record of contact with Jekyll exists, but, in all likelihood, he would have known of her work and the artful juxtaposition of flower colors she advocated. After all, Monet was a serious horticulturist, with his own deep interest in color schemes in his garden.

The other giant in the world of English gardening at this time, who was turning Victorian-patterned, bedding-out style on its head, was Jekyll's friend William Robinson (1838–1935). They first met in 1875 and maintained a friendship and working relationship for fifty years. Robinson advocated a wilder cottage garden style, one that recognized the forms and colors of flowering perennials, a school of thinking that Monet would in all likelihood have been aware of through Robinson's books, *The Wild Garden* (1870) and *The English Flower Garden* (1883).

By 1866, at age twenty-six, Monet was already capturing the attention of the Parisian art world, but even then he was living at the edge of poverty. He married Camille-Léonie Doncieux, a painter's model, in 1870, and shortly thereafter, their son Jean and a later son Michel were born. Between 1870 and 1871, during the Franco-Prussian War, Monet and family moved to London with Camille Pissarro, where Monet studied the works of J. M. W. Turner (1775–1851), an important disseminator of information on color theory, and John Constable (1776–1837), whose paintings helped clarify Monet's understanding of color. This was also the year that Robinson launched his magazine, *The Garden,* in London, and which Jekyll contributed to and later edited for a few years.

Monet returned to France in late 1871 to live and work from a rented home in Argenteuil, a village on the Seine near Paris, where artist Georges Braque's father was Monet's carpenter. Monet planted his first garden at Argenteuil (figure 7.1).

Beset by financial setbacks, the Monets were forced to move into the home of Ernest and Alice Hoschede, important patrons, in Vetheuil in 1878. Given Monet's wife Camille's grave illness, Alice took over the rearing of his two boys. Camille died the following year. Upon the death of Ernest Hoschede a few years later, Alice and Monet continued to live together for another ten years or so before marrying. In 1883, with their finances somewhat improved, they rented the home at Giverny in Normandy but did not start gardening immediately. Seven years later, with the growing success of his work, Monet purchased Giverny and started excavation for the water lily pond. In a permit application to the municipal authorities in Vernon, he wrote that he wanted to create the pond "with a view to motifs for painting." At one point, during the forty-three years he worked on the garden, he also wrote, "Everything I have earned has gone into these gardens." One story has it that on a particularly cold winter night, Monet feared that the heating system in his greenhouse for orchids might fail. If it did, he wanted to know; he and his family slept in the greenhouse that night.

Another important change taking place in the English and European art worlds was a new exploration of color theory, a fact that was not lost on Jekyll, who, as mentioned before, published *Colour Schemes for the Flower Garden* in 1908. In 1839, one year before Monet was born, a French industrial chemist, Michel Eugène Chevreul, was working for a pigment manufacturing company. He researched how to create keener brightness for the color range of synthetic pigments his company produced. He published those findings in *The Law of Simultaneous Color Contrast*. It was widely circulated across Europe, especially among artists.

Fig. 7.1: Claude Monet (1840–1926), *The Flower Garden,* ca. 1866 (Argenteuil, France), in the collection of the Musée d'Orsay, Paris, France, photo credit Reunion des Musées Nationaux/Art Resource, New York, photograph by Herve Lewandowski. The relationship between house and garden was important to Monet. Here, windows afforded a view from house into garden.

Figure 7.1: Monet's house and garden at Giverny, 2001, photograph by Karen Bussolini. Along the entire back façade of Monet's home at Giverny, doors give rise to garden paths; windows provide view lines deep into this linear garden, one whose lines lay perpendicular to the house. One complements the other.

One of Monet's first urges when he arrived at Giverny was to grow flowers that he could paint in still lifes when inclement weather prevented him from painting outdoors. These still lifes were preceded, however, by paintings of women in gardens; later, he focused on painting the gardens themselves. In many ways, he planted flowering perennials and annuals in order to more fully understand color, something that artist Leslie Parke explores on pages 155 to 157. (By way of an aside, the house at Giverny gained its signature pink color when the house painter from Guadeloupe that Monet had hired ground up brick in the whitewash to remind the house painter of his own home among the French islands in the eastern Caribbean.)

Monet next began to explore painting in series—haystacks, the façade of Rouen Cathedral, poplars, water lilies, or the Epte River at different times of the day. Between 1883 and 1908, he traveled to the Mediterranean to paint a series in Venice, and later he returned to England to paint a series of works showing the changing light on the Houses of Parliament and Charing Cross Bridge.

His wife, Alice, died in 1911, his son Jean in 1914. Monet died in 1926 and is buried in the Giverny churchyard. He once wrote, "I want the unobtainable. Other artists paint a bridge, a house, a boat . . . I want to paint the air which surrounds the bridge, the house, the boat . . . and that is nothing short of impossible."

Leslie Parke is a painter working in New York State. After graduating with a BA and MA in art

Figure 7.2: Claude Monet (1840–1926), *Water Lilies*, 1904, in the collection of the Musée des Beaux-Arts, Andre Malraux, Le Havre, France, photo credit Reunion des Musées Nationaux/Art Resource, New York, photographed by C. Jean. In a permit application to the authorities in Vernon, Monet said he wanted to excavate for the lily pond "with a view to motifs for painting."

Figure 7.2A: The lily pond at Giverny, 2001, photograph by Karen Bussolini. The lily pond has been expertly restored and now appears as it did when Monet was living at Giverny.

Figure 7.3: Leslie Parke, *Lily Pond,* used with permission from the artist. In 1994, artist Parke lived across the road from Monet's Giverny for five months. Each day she painted or photographed the recently restored gardens and lily pond there.

from Bennington College, she worked on television documentaries but shortly thereafter turned to full-time work as a painter. Over more than twenty years, she has established an international reputation with exhibits in America, Europe, and South America, as well as gallery representation in Toronto and San Diego. In 1994, she received a Lila Wallace–Reader's Digest Artist-in-Residence Grant to live and paint at the Claude Monet Foundation in Giverny. She now lives in New York State, where she has painted all the walls of the rooms in her second-story apartment with passages from Bonnard's paintings.

## COMMENTS BY LESLIE PARKE, A CONTEMPORARY ARTIST, ON MONET, HIS GARDENS, AND PAINTINGS

In 1975, while visiting London, I found Mathew Dunbar's book of historic photos of Monet at Giverny. This was the beginning of my intense interest in Monet's gardens, which, at the time, were still almost nine years from being restored. As I was flipping through this book in London in 1975, large trees were growing up through the skylights of Monet's studio in Giverny; the house had been ransacked, the garden was a collection of weeds, and wisteria had fallen into the polluted pond.

In 1994, I saw the restored Giverny for the first time. With the restoration, however, came the tourists, and with the tourists came the books, postcards, posters, magnets, mugs, and scarves. The gardens, once obscured by neglect, were now obscured by overexposure. Was it even possible to experience the gardens as Monet had, to understand the relationship between his art and his garden, and was there a way that a contemporary artist such as myself could interact with the garden that didn't smack of Monet-lite?

Thanks to the artist-in-residence grant, I spent five months during 1994 living across the street from Monet's house. I was given keys to the garden, which afforded me unlimited access. I spent hours floating in the green rowboat that appears in several of Monet's paintings. I ate dinner on the second floor of the house overlooking the gardens and played *boule* with the guards. Once the gates to the garden were closed to the public, I cooked alfresco in the garden. I was able to experience the gardens in an intimate way.

I arrived in June 1994; the wisteria had already bloomed and passed. We were in high summer, and while the English garden was filled with bloom, the pond was a sea of reflected green from the surrounding shrubs and trees, the sky barely visible through the leaves. The pond remained that way for weeks, with little modulation in the color and certainly nothing of what I had seen in Monet's water lily paintings. I began to think that he had made the whole thing up, a complete fabrication having nothing to do with what was before him.

It turned out that to see Giverny and the gardens as Monet had would take time. So, as I returned to the gardens each day at different times, in different weather, and finally as the seasons changed, I began to see the place as it had appeared in Monet's paintings. But I didn't fully understand the genius of his work or the profound accuracy of his eye until one morning I arose before dawn. I followed a path along the Epte River, a tributary of the Seine that runs through Giverny, to see the sunrise over the river. Finally, I came upon a spot that had all the characterization of his Epte paintings. I set up my camera and took pictures of the same motif every minute or so. As I did, one after another of his paintings revealed themselves to me.

As I watched the sunrise over the river, I came to understand things in his paintings that hadn't made sense to me before: that the trees on the left were lighter in his paintings because they were being dissolved by the sun as it rose; that the paintings of the earliest part of the day were light and muted as the fog sat heavily over the water and the low light streamed through it, but an hour later, when the sun was at its apex, the river and surrounding trees were inky black.

The most startling realization was that the images that appear in this series of paintings are of changes of light and atmosphere that occurred every five minutes during a single hour in the morning. To perceive the change without the aid of a camera is an extraordinary

achievement. To capture that phenomenon on canvas, something that would entail hours of work done over many days, seems equally impossible. For me, it was the moment I understood Monet's genius; I was able to experience Monet's eye in real time.

Monet spent forty-three years living in Giverny and didn't start to paint the gardens until he lived there for ten years. What could I accomplish in five months? My first urge was to resist anything Monet. Instead of light and color in the garden, I concentrated on the structure and tonality. I worked on shaped canvases and played with shapes derived from the bridge and the green rowboat. Even while undertaking this, I observed the garden every day, particularly the lily pond. By the end of my stay, I was seduced by all things Monet—the light, the color, and the atmosphere.

Monet's "grand decorations," the murals of the lily pond that hang in two oval galleries in the Musée de L'Orangerie in Paris, are the culmination of his achievement as both an artist and a gardener. It makes sense that his vision that had so accurately recorded what lay between his eye and the landscape for more than sixty years would finally turn inward. The pond became a window to his soul. It is finally here that Monet merges with his subject matter.

While still at Giverny, I made paintings mostly of the lily pond (see figure 7.3). These paintings are large scale. The lily flowers, for example, might be four times as large as the ones in the garden. The scale imposes a sense of the physicality of the paint. Finally, and this is where Monet reenters my work, the quality of light is important to me. While he could record the light of the very atmosphere, I want to record the light so that it feels as though it is emanating from the canvas.

My research into Monet turned up the fact that he created what were variously known as *les tombes,* or paint boxes. These were gardens roughly 4 x 7 feet in which he planted different combinations of flowering perennials and annuals over many growing seasons in order to observe how color combinations changed under constantly changing light and atmospheric conditions as the sun passed overhead. He also experimented by stippling in white flowers among combinations of flowers in reds, yellows, and blues, for example, to see how the white dots caused the other colors to vibrate. As far as I know, there are no paintings of the paint boxes. I believe he planted them to help train his eye. We have to remember that there would not be other possibilities to make these observations—he had to see them in nature. He couldn't turn to a computer and the Internet to research color. Even with the new paints that were being created during that century, it would not be easy to create the vivid quality of color he could get with flowers. It is only in nature that he would have had the chance to observe light passing through color, which he could do, for example, by looking at a petal that is backlit.

In the end, it was exactly this that stayed with me from my experience at Giverny. I looked for Monet's light and color in the garden. And then I tried to analyze how I could achieve that quality in paint. I was using his garden in the same way that he was using his paint box beds. For me, it had very little to do with composition. The gardens turned out to be a color and light laboratory for me. That was not what I was looking for in the garden when I first arrived. But when I gave myself over to them in different times of the day and in different seasons, I grew immeasurably as a painter. Monet didn't paint anything in the garden until he had lived there for ten years. I painted the garden right away, but I didn't understand it until after studying it for ten years.

*The Russian Doll* by Richard Schmid.

# FLORAL ARRANGEMENTS: ART IN BLOOM

Art in Bloom, a nationwide celebration of fine art and floral arranging, started in 1976, at the Museum of Fine Arts in Boston. The idea, first developed by Charles Thomas, was to not only celebrate the museum and floral designers in the Boston area but also to encourage museum attendance in early spring. Within five years, the program had expanded to a four-day event. In late April 1995, I gave a lecture on fine art as inspiration for garden design at the Museum of Fine Art's Art in Bloom lecture series, a lecture that, thanks to Gibbs Smith, has blossomed into this book. By 1997, over twenty thousand visitors were coming to Boston for the event. During the meteoric expansion of the first Art in Bloom in Boston, the idea began to spread to art museums across the country.

The idea behind Art in Bloom is to interpret a painting with a floral design that is placed adjacent to the artwork. In some museums, the director of the program assigns artworks to various floral designers or garden clubs, while in others designers choose their own artworks to interpret. Museum organizers encourage anywhere from forty to one hundred and fifty floral designers to create arrangements to be set next to that many works of art. The art must never be overwhelmed by the flowers.

Floral designers take into account the subject matter of the work of art as well as the time period in which it was created. Mood, light, color, scale, line, pattern, proportion, and a balance among all these elements are central to the challenge of creating just the right floral arrangement to complement the art. Timing is everything. As one floral designer said, "You need sharp scissors and a fast car!"

In 1996, writer Victoria Jane Ream, from Salt Lake City, Utah, who is also an accomplished gardener, combined forces with Norwegian photographer Sjur Fedje to document Art in Bloom as practiced across America. After a year of research, they traveled nationwide, interviewing and photographing the work of floral designers as displayed in art museums. The result is a magnificent 270-page book, *Art in Bloom*. Read this book and follow artist Paul Klee's advice: "The eye follows the roads, which are laid down for it in the work of art." Ream's book will show you how to develop your own "art in bloom" in your home as well as how to appreciate what you see when you attend Art in Bloom in a museum holding this event.

## Figure 8.1

### Materials:

Delphinium: *Delphinium* x cv.
Transvaal daisy: *Gerbera jamesonii*
Lily: *Lilium* sp.
Daylily: *Hemerocallis* cv.
Siberian iris: *Iris sibirica*
African lily: *Agapanthus* sp.

**Floral designer note:** This portrait evokes a feeling of charm and open generosity with a touch of Oriental mystery. I chose fruits as well as flowers to represent these qualities. I chose the luscious red fruits to bring out the warmth of the reds in the painting as well as to suggest a sense of abundance and concern for the temporal. I selected the flowers to reflect the rich color of Countess Schouvaloff's alluring apparel with the Oriental lilies suggesting the exotic.

**About the artist:** Vigee-LeBrun was a celebrated painter of the late eighteenth and early nineteenth centuries. She produced close to eight hundred portraits in the course of her long career. As painter to Marie Antoinette, she was forced to leave France at the outbreak of the Revolution in 1789. During an extended visit to Russia from 1795 to 1801, she painted many of the Russian aristocracy, including this one.

## Figure 8.2

### Materials:

African lily: *Agapanthus* spp.
Astilbe: *Astilbe* x *arendsii*
Delphinium: *Delphinium elatum*
Prairie gentian: *Eustoma* x *grandiflora*
Hydrangea: *Hydrangea macrophylla*
Casablanca Lily: *Lilium* x 'Casablanca'
Fantasy rose: *Rosa* x 'Fantasy'
Ruscus: *Ruscus hypoglossum*
Soapwort: *Saponaria officinalis*

**Floral design note:** The goal was to capture the freshness and vitality of the painting. The white lilies, as well as the apron and pitcher, move the viewer's focus between the canvas and the flowers. The child's softness is enhanced by the full-blossomed hydrangeas and the cascading soapwort. A variety of shades of green in foliage and flower repeat the background colors of the painting.

**About the artist:** Cassatt was born in Allegheny City, Pennsylvania, now Pittsburgh. Both parents were from wealthy banking families. Before the age of ten, she had visited most of the major European cities. She studied art at the Academy of Fine Arts in Philadelphia from 1861 to 1865 and in 1866 moved to Paris. She studied with Camille Pissarro in 1872. In 1874, she met Edgar Degas, who invited her, the only woman artist, to show her art with him and the other impressionists in 1879. She never married, yet the vast majority of her paintings record the tender, intimate relationship between mother and child. In 1904, France awarded her the Legion of Honor. She died in 1926 at Château de Beaufresne, near Paris.

Figure 8.1: Marie Louise Elizabeth Vigee-LeBrun (1755–1842), *Portrait of the Young Countess Schouvaloff,* 1797, at the University of Utah Museum of Fine Arts. Floral design by Kristine McGhie, Salt Lake City, Utah. The color red, in its many shades and tints in flower, fruit, painting, and rosy marble, unifies this sumptuous arrangement. Blue and white provide the contrast to intensify reds.

Figure 8.2: Mary Cassatt (1844–1926), *Patty-Cake,* 1897, Denver Museum of Art and Botanic Garden, floral design by Barbara Baldwin and Georgia Grey, the Garden Club of Denver. The purity and innocence of the color white draws table, apron, floral arrangement, and painting into a gently unified whole. Dark greens and blue greens provide the contrast that heightens the white.

# *Appendixes*

## Appendix A: Internet Research Gathered around the Crosscurrents between Paintings and Garden Design

*Google these painters to see images of gardens they have painted. In many cases, you can gain quite specific information regarding design, layout, or plant combinations that you can apply to your own garden:*

Helen Allingham, English (1848–1926)
Frank A. Bicknell, American (1866–1943)
William Chadwick, American (1879–1962)
John Constable, English (1776–1837), especially the
   Flower Garden series he painted between 1814 and
   1816
Gaines Ruger Donoho, American (1857–1916)
George Samuel Elgood, English (1851–1943)
Lydia Field Emmet, American (1866–1952)
Alexis Jean Fournier, American (1865–1948)
Abbott Fuller Graves, American (1859–1936)
Philip Leslie Hale, American (1865–1931)
Childe Hassam, American (1859–1935)
David Inshaw, English (1943– )
Gustav Klimt, Austrian (1862–1918)
Edouard Manet, French (1823–1883)
Henri Martin, French (1860–1943)
Willard Leroy Metcalf, American (1858–1925)
Claude Monet, French (1840–1926)
Alfred Parsons, American, painting in England
   (1847–1920)
Beatrice Parsons, English (1870–1955)
Camille Pissarro, French (1830–1903)
Humphrey Repton, English (1752–1818)
Peter Paul Rubens, Flemish (1577–1640)
P. A. Rysbrack, English (1684–1748)
John Singer Sargent, American (1856–1925)
Stanley Spencer, English (1891–1959)
David Suff, English (1955– )
Louis Turpin, English (1947– )
John Henry Twachtman, American (1853–1902)
Vincent van Gogh, Dutch (1835–1890)
Edouard Vuillard, French (1868–1940)
Margaret Waterfield, English (1860–1950)
Theodore Wores, American (1859–1939)

*See these other references for more information:*

Anthony Huxley's *The Painted Garden: The Garden through the
   Artist's Eye;* Wellfleet Press, 1988.
Medieval gardens depicted in *The Book of Hours* or *Opus
   Ruralium Commodorum,* the source book for gardening
   and agriculture, completed in 1305.
Thirteenth-century Japanese and Chinese prints and
   scrolls depicting Eastern gardens and landscapes in
   Guillaume de Lorris' *The Romaunt de la Rose.*

*Google these contemporary artists who are working or who have worked
during the last hundred years. These are landscape painters, painters of
gardens, and still-life painters with special interest in flowers:*

Kathy Anderson
John Barkley
Dennis Miller Bunker
Bobbie Burgers
Darlene Cole
Lois Dodd
Joan Elliott
Nancy Guzik
Childe Hassam
Alex Katz
Hagop Keledjian
Norman Laliberte
Robert Marchessault
John McCormick
Tim Merrett
Leslie Parke
Daniele Rochon
Richard Schmid
Dennis Sheehan
Neil Welliver

*Google British artists who have created their own gardens:*

Ian Hamilton Finlay
Barbara Hepworth
Patrick Heron
Ivon Hitchens
Edward Atkinson Hornel
Derek Jarman
Charles Mahoney

Cedric Morris
Alfred Parsons
James Tissot
See *Art of the Garden*, Nicholas Alfrey et al, Tate Modern
    Catalogue, London, 2005.

*See Web sites showing a wide range of art:*

aaa.si.edu/home.cfm (Smithsonian Archives of American
    Art)
abcgallery.com (an online art museum)
abstractart.20m.com
art.com
artchive.com
artcyclopedia.com
artincontext.com
artlex.com (art dictionary)
artnet.com
artprice.com
artres.com (Art Resource)
askart.com
fada.com (Fine Art Dealers Association)
fineamericanart.com
fineoldart.com
halter.net (online art museum)
paletaworld.org
peterjungfineart.com (nineteenth- and twentieth-century
    American and European art; much of the collection is
    of landscapes)
usartists.org
villageartsofputney.com

*Google specific art museums, and then, once at the homepage of the Web
site, narrow your search to find work by specific artists or styles:*

The Chicago Art Institute
The Louvre
The Metropolitan Museum of Art
The National Gallery of Art

*Google a specific artist:*

Place the artist's name in the search box and then add the
word "artist" after it to avoid calling up people in other
fields by the same name.

## Appendix B: Symbolism and Associations in Art and Gardens

Objects in the garden, as in paintings, can embody personal as well as universal associations and meaning. If you put sculptures or objects in your garden that have broad, almost universal meaning—for example, a cast-stone pineapple as a symbol of welcome—those objects resonate with meaning. Other objects—your grandmother's stone birdbath or a large seashell that you brought back from a special vacation—have personal meaning limited to a close circle of family and friends. Even though all the associations of the vacation may not be understood by those who visit your garden, every visitor will feel the tug of the ocean when they see that large shell.

Sometimes a particularly well-chosen object can carry both personal associations as well as universal meaning. As Mary and I were developing our garden in Vermont, we installed three topiary life-size frames of an ewe and two lambs in the garden. For Mary and me, those three objects in the garden remind us of the sheep farm on which Mary grew up in England. Others might see the lambs as symbols of the Lamb of God. That is, the depth of meaning of objects all depends on your past experience, your knowledge, and emotions. Choose objects for your garden, just as painters choose what objects to include in their paintings, and your garden will take on deeper meaning and more varied emotions. In other words, you can speak to your visitors through symbolic objects, many of which have taken on deeper religious or cultural meaning over the centuries. They have become broadly recognized symbols, many of which painters, and gardeners, include in their work to carry abstract meaning in a physical object. (If you read *The DaVinci Code*, you know something about Christian symbolism.)

Following are some of the symbols that have broad universal meaning that you can incorporate into your garden. (For a more complete picture of symbols and their meaning, refer to *Nature and Its Symbols* by Lucia Impelluso, as I did for parts of these lists.) To find other symbols, simply Google key words such as "nature symbols," "plant symbols," or "color symbolism," or visit www.colormatters.com or www.writedesignonline.com.

## Symbolism and Plants

These specific plants can carry a new level of meaning in your garden.

Apple: Temptation and redemption, symbol of the fall of man

Bamboo: Longevity

Carnation: Betrothal and marriage

Chrysanthemums: The national symbol of Japan, long life

Columbine: The dove, the Holy Spirit

Daisies: Innocence

Fig: Fertility, well-being, tree of knowledge of good and evil, lust

Flowers: Signs of heaven and an unfolding spiritual life

Forget-me-not and rosemary: Remembrance

Gourd: Attribute of wayfarers, resurrection, salvation

Grape vine: Symbol of Bacchus, god of wine, or The Eucharist and Christ, who said, "I am the true vine."

Ivy: Eternal love and fidelity

Lemon: Fidelity in love, salvation, curative

Lily of the valley: Humility, purity

Lily: Purity, female fecundity

Narcissus: Self-adoration, or, in Christian iconography, the triumph of divine love over death and egotism

Oaks: Physical and moral strength

Orchid: Perfection

Peach: The fruit of salvation, truth

Pear: Well-being, the sweetness of virtue

Plum: Fidelity, charity, humility

Pomegranate: Resurrection, chastity, fertility, concord, and conservation

Quince: Love, fertility, marriage, symbol of resurrection

Rose (red): Love, passion

Rose (white): Purity, innocence

Rose of Sharon: Christ's mother, Mary

Sage: Virtue

Strawberry: Earthly paradise, innocence, humility

Sunflower: Devotion, infatuation

Thistle: Symbol of Scotland

Tulip: Love

Violet: Faithfulness, humility, chastity

## Symbolic Animals, Birds, and Insects

Garden ornaments and plaques that include any of the following can lend another level of meaning to your garden.

Bee: Industriousness, diligence, chastity

Butterfly: The beauty of nature, the female, beneficence, the soul

Cat: Liberty, hunter, conflict

Dog: Fidelity, devotion

Dolphin: Faith, gentle disposition

Donkey: Humility, meekness, simplicity, laziness

Dove: Peace, innocence, purity

Eagle: Power, pride, victory, intellect, sight

Elephant: Temperance, wisdom, strength, docility

Ermine: Purity, chastity, resurrection, symbol of the sense of touch

Goldfinch: The human soul, an amulet against disease

Horse: Vitality, victory, pride

Lamb: Innocence, humility, patience, meekness, symbol of Christ

Lion: Virility, strength, fortitude

Owl: Knowledge, wisdom, night

Ox: Patience, fortitude, strength

Peacock: Resurrection, immortality, arrogance, pride

Pelican: Charity, piety, good nature

Rabbit: Venus, fecundity

Rooster: Vigilance

Sphinx (woman's head, lion's body): Enigma, attribute of the Nile River

Swallow: Resurrection and spring, gives light back

Swan: Love, purity, virtue

Unicorn: Purity, chastity, virginity

## Symbolic Objects in a Garden

Include various symbolic shapes in the form of bed or lawn shapes or stone paving to carry these symbolic meanings into your garden. As in a painting, visual symbols can quietly carry much meaning. Turn to Carl Liungman's *Dictionary of Symbols* for hundreds of symbols that you could place in the ground at the junction of paths, in stone terraces and sitting areas, and even as objects hung on walls. Painters also use these same objects and shapes, sometimes for symbolic effect, sometimes to add the shape to their work.

"8" positioned horizontally: Infinity, endlessness

Circle with a horizontal/vertical cross in it: From the Bronze Age—thunder, highest power, respect

Circle with a dot in the center: The sun, annual plants in botany, the archangel

Circle with two dots in the center set horizontally: Biennial plants

Circle: The sun, completeness, cycles, the eye

Crescent: The powers of the moon, reflective, receptive

Diamond: Courage, daring

Egg: Birth, potential

Heart: Love

Hexagram (six-pointed star with crossing lines): The Jewish Kingdom

Maltese cross: The eight points symbolize the eight virtues of knights—loyalty, piety, generosity, courage, modesty, contempt of death, helpfulness toward the poor, respect for the church

Oval: All eternity, all time, all possibilities

Pentacle (five-pointed star with crossing lines): The human being—head, two arms, two legs

Spiral, clockwise: Water, power, independent movement

Spiral, counterclockwise: Return, homecoming, the home

Square: Elemental earth, ground, land

Triangle, downward pointing: Stability, Holy Trinity, the chalice, female, water, passive element

Triangle, upward pointing: Aspiration, rising up, the blade, male, Holy Trinity

Two overlapping circles: Togetherness, intimate relationship

Yin-yang sign: Yin, passive, receiving, malleable; yang, energy, activity, spirit

## Color Symbolism in Western Culture

Black: Aloof, unknown, power, sophistication, formality, elegance, wealth, evil, depth, remorse, mournful, threatening, deliberate

Blue: Peace, tranquility, sky, harmony, unity, confidence, water, cleanliness, introspected, calming, moral, downcast, gloomy,

Brown: Earthy, health, home, comfort, endurance, stability, simplicity

Gold: Royalty, the color of the heavens, fields of grain

Gray: Security, reliability, intelligence, staid, conservative, dignity, solidity

Green: Nature, environment, health, good luck, youth, renewal, vigor, spring, unripe, unsophisticated, leaves and foliage and thus life

Orange: Energy, balance, warmth, vibrant, flamboyant, demanding attention, creative, adventurous, sociable; in Ireland, the color of the Protestants

Pink: Childish innocence, good health and life, purity

Purple: Royalty, spirituality, nobility, ceremony, wisdom, beauty, princely, exalted, arrogance, mystery

Red: Excitement, energy, passion, strength, fire, blood, intensity, outspoken

White: Reverence, purity, simplicity, cleanliness, peace, humility, innocence, snow, empty, blank, honorable, harmless, dependable

Yellow: Joy, happiness, optimism, sunshine, hope; also jealousy, deceit

## Color Symbolism in Eastern and Middle Eastern Cultures

Blue: China, immortality; Jews, holiness; Middle East, protective

Green: India, the color of Islam; some tropical countries, danger

Red: China, luck, celebration; India, purity (color of wedding dresses); Asian cultures, signifies joy when combined with white

Saffron: Hindu cultures, the sacred color

White: Eastern cultures, mourning, death; Japan, white carnations signify death

Yellow: Asia, sacred, imperial

## Appendix C: Language, Gardens, and Paintings

### Words to Describe a Garden, Landscape, or Painting

When you have the language to clearly describe what you see or how you feel about a painting or garden, that language helps you clarify your reaction to it. That language, in turn, may help as you design a garden around one of these words—dramatic, comforting, intense—or avoid the pitfalls implied in the word—floundering, predictable, piecemeal. Use these adjectives in your analysis of a garden you are visiting, a garden you want to create, or a painting you admire. This list is inspired by and based on a list by Dave Jacke in *Edible Forest Gardens:*

abstract
active
affected
airy
aloof
anachronistic
animated
approachable
arbitrary
archetypal
architectural
arranged
artful
artificial
atmospheric
authentic
awesome
axial
banal
botanical
bright
calculated
calm
cautious
challenging
chaotic
charming
classical
claustrophobic
clean
colorful
comforting
commercial

composed
conservative
contradictory
conventional
cool
cozy
cramped
crisp
curious
curvy
dainty
damp
dark
dazzling
decorative
deep
delightful
dense
derivative
designed
dignified
distant
distinguished
disturbing
dramatic
dreamy/dreamlike
dull
dynamic
eccentric
edgy
elaborate
elegant
emotional

enchanting
enclosed
engaging
episodic
evocative
exalting
exciting
exotic
expansive
extensive
extravagant
exuberant
fanciful
fashionable
feminine
flat
floundering
flowing
fluid
forestlike
formal
fragmented
fresh
futuristic
gentle
geometric
gestural
graceful
grand
green
hard
harmonious
heroic
hidden
hilly
historical
humorous
impenetrable
impressionistic
incoherent
inconsistent
informal
inhabited
innovative
insipid
inspired
inspiring
instinctual

insular
intense
intimate
intimidating
introspective
inventive
invigorating
inviting
isolated
jarring
labored
landscaped
light
linear
lofty
luxuriant
magical
majestic
masculine
minimalist
monotonous
monumental
moving
muted
mysterious
natural
naturalistic
nervous
nestled
noisy
nostalgic
obsessive
open
orderly
ordinary
overgrown
overpowering
overworked
panoramic
pastoral
peaceful
personal
physical
picturesque
piecemeal
pinched
placid
playful

| | |
|---|---|
| pleasant | spontaneous |
| predictable | startling |
| presented | stately |
| private | static |
| profound | steep |
| provocative | stiff |
| quiet | stolid |
| radiant | stony |
| raw | straight |
| real/honest | stuffy |
| refined | stylized |
| relaxing | subtle |
| renewing | suburban |
| restrained | sumptuous |
| rhythmic | sunny |
| rich | sustainable |
| robust | synthetic |
| rocky | technical |
| rolling | tense |
| romantic | theatrical |
| rough | thoughtful |
| rugged | timeless |
| rural | towering |
| sacred | traditional |
| sculptural | tranquil |
| secluded | uncomfortable |
| self absorbed | undulating |
| self-conscious | unified |
| sensuous | uniform |
| serene | unkempt |
| serious | unpleasant |
| shadowy | unselfconscious |
| shady | unspoiled |
| sheltered | untamed |
| sheltering | urban |
| simple | varied |
| sloping | vast |
| smooth | visionary |
| soaring | warm |
| sober | well maintained |
| soft | wet |
| somber | whimsical |
| sophisticated | wild |
| soulful | windswept |
| soulless | witty |
| spare | woodsy |
| sparse | |
| spiritual | |

## Words That Describe Emotions Elicited by a Garden, Landscape, or Painting

| | |
|---|---|
| abandoned | enclosed |
| ambiguous | envious |
| anger | exhausted |
| annoyed | exposed |
| awed | fascinated |
| betrayed | fearful |
| bored | frantic |
| burdened | gratified |
| calm | happy |
| captivated | humbled |
| challenged | hurt |
| charmed | ignored |
| childish | inspired |
| confused | intimidated |
| constrained | isolated |
| contented | nostalgic |
| defeated | overwhelmed |
| delighted | peaceful |
| diminished | precarious |
| distracted | pressured |
| disturbed | protected |
| dominated | refreshed |
| dubious | relieved |
| eager | secure |
| elated | tense |
| electrified | unsettled |
| enchanted | vulnerable |

# Bibliography

## Books Related to Art and Artists

Adler, Kathleen, et al. *Americans in Paris 1860–1900.* National Gallery Company: London, 2006.

Alfrey, Nicholas, et al, editors. *Art of the Garden: The Garden in British Art, 1800 to the Present Day.* Tate Publishing: London, 2004.

Barnes, Dr. Albert C., and the Barnes Foundation. *Great French Paintings from the Barnes Foundation: Impressionist, Post-Impressionist, and Early Modern.* Alfred A. Knopf: New York, 2001.

Baxandall, Michael. *Painting & Experience in Fifteenth-Century Italy: A Primer in the Social History of Pictorial Style.* Oxford University Press: Oxford, 1972.

Bumpus, Judith: *Impressionist Gardens.* Phaidon, New York, 1990.

Ebony, David. *Emily Mason: The Fifth Element.* George Braziller: New York, 2006.

Elderfield, John. *Henri Matisse: A Retrospective.* The Museum of Modern Art: New York, 1992.

Halpern, Daniel, editor. *Writers on Artists,* North Point Press: San Francisco, 1988.

Heffernan, James A.W. *The Recreation of Landscape: A Study of Wordsworth, Coleridge, Constable, and Turner.* University Press of New England: Hanover, NH, 1985.

Ives, Colta, et al. *Vincent Van Gogh: The Drawings.* The Metropolitan Museum of Art: New York, 2005.

Jacke, Dave. *Edible Forest Gardens: The Ecology and Design for Home Scale Food Forests.* Chelsea Green Press: White River Junction, VT, 2005.

Johns, Elizabeth. *Paths to Impressionism: French and American Landscape Paintings from The Worcester Art Museum.* Worcester, Massachusetts, Art Museum, 2003.

Kunitz, Stanley, et al. *The Wild Braid: A Poet Reflects on a Century in the Garden.* W. W. Norton: New York, 2005.

Liungman, Carl G. *Dictionary of Symbols.* ABC-CLIO Books, Santa Barbara, 1991.

McClatchy, J. D., editor. *Poets on Painters: Essays on the Art of Painting by Twentieth-Century Poets.* University of California Press: Berkeley, 1988.

Orr, Lynn Federle, et al. *Monet: Late Paintings of Giverny from the Musée Marmottan.* Harry N. Abrams: New York, 1995.

Schulze, Sabine, editor. *The Painter's Garden: Design, Inspiration, Delight.* Hatje Cantz Publishers: Ostfildern, Germany, 2006. (The catalogue was in support of the exhibit by the same name at the Stadel Museum, Frankfurt am Main, Germany, 2006.)

Smith, Valerie, et al. *Down the Garden Path: The Artist's Garden after Modernism.* Queens Museum of Art: New York, 2005.

Spring, Justin. *Wolf Kahn.* Harry N. Abrams, New York, 1996.

Watkins, Nicholas. *Bonnard.* Phaidon Press: London, 1994.

Wittmer, Pierre. *Caillebotte and His Garden at Yerres.* Harry N. Abrams: New York, 1991.

## Painting and Composition in Art

Payne, Edgar. *Composition of Outdoor Painting.* DeRu's Fine Arts: Bellflower, CA, 2005.

Schmid, Richard. *Alla Prima: Everything I know About Painting.* Stove Prairie Press: South Burlington, VT, 1999.

## Landscape and Gardens

Bradley-Hole, Christopher. *The Minimalist Garden.* Mitchell Beazley, London, 1999.

Bye, A. E. *Art into Landscape, Landscape into Art.* PDA Publishers: Mesa, Arizona, 1983.

Dash, Robert. *Notes from Madoo: Making a Garden in the Hamptons.* Houghton Mifflin: Boston, 2000.

Eck, Joe. *Elements of Garden Design.* North Point Press: New York, 2005.

Eddison, Sydney, and Steve Silk. *Gardens to Go: Creating and Designing a Container Garden.* Bulfinch Press: New York, 2005.

Farrand, Beatrix. *The Bulletins of Reef Point Gardens.* Sagapress: Sagaponack, NY, 1997.

Fell, Derek. *Cézanne's Garden.* Simon & Schuster: New York, 2004.

———. *Secrets of Monet's Garden: Bringing the Beauty of Monet's Style to Your Own Garden.* Metrobooks: New York, 2001.

———. *The Impressionist Garden.* Frances Lincoln: London, 2006.

Gordon, Robert, and Sydney Eddison. *Monet The Gardener.* Universe Publishing: Lincoln, NE, 2002.

Hartlage, Richard. *Bold Visions for the Garden: Basics, Magic & Inspiration.* Fulcrum Publishing, Golden, CO, 2001.

Hayward, Gordon. *Garden Paths: Inspiring Designs and Practical Projects.* Firefly Books, Ontario, Canada, 1997.

———. *The Intimate Garden: Twenty Years and Four Seasons in Our Garden.* W. W. Norton: New York, 2005.

———. *The Welcoming Garden: Designing Your Own Front Garden.* Gibbs Smith, Publisher: Salt Lake City, 2006.

————. *Your House, Your Garden: A Foolproof Approach to Garden Design.* W. W. Norton: New York, 2003.

Levy, Leah. *Peter Walker: Minimalist Gardens.* Spacemaker Press: Washington, D.C., 1997.

Rose, Graham. *The Romantic Garden.* Frances Lincoln: London, 2006.

Rose, James. *The Heavenly Environment.* New City Cultural Services: Hong Kong, 1987.

Snow, Marc (aka James Rose). *Modern American Gardens— Designed by James Rose.* Reinhold Publishing: New York, 1967.

Strong, Sir Roy. *Creating Formal Gardens.* Little, Brown & Company: Boston, 1990.

Thaxter, Celia. *An Island Garden.* Kessinger Publishing: Whitefish, MT, 2007.

Whaley, Emily, and William Baldwin. *Mrs. Whaley and Her Charleston Garden.* Fireside: Wichita, KS, 1998.

Willsdon, Clare A. P. *In The Gardens of Impressionism.* Vendome Press: New York, 2004.

### Color

Eddison, Sydney. *The Gardener's Color Wheel: A Guide to Using Color in the Garden.* The Color Wheel Company: Philomath, OR, 2006.

————. *The Gardener's Palette: Creating Color in the Garden.* Contemporary Books: New York, 2003.

Hobhouse, Penelope. *Color in Your Garden.* Little Brown & Company: Boston, 1985.

Jekyll, Gertrude. *Colour Schemes for the Flower Garden.* Antique Collectors' Club: Easthampton, MA, 1986.

Lawson, Andrew. *The Gardener's Book of Colour.* Frances Lincoln: London, 2006.

Ream, Victoria Jane. *Art in Bloom.* Deseret Equity, Publishing Division: Salt Lake City, 1997.

Sheldon, Elisabeth. *The Flamboyant Garden.* Henry Holt & Company: New York, 1997.

Williams, Paul. *Garden Colour Palette.* Conran Octopus: London, 2000.

### Connecting Gardens to Art

Hill, May Brawley. *On Foreign Soil: American Gardeners Abroad.* Harry N. Abrams: New York, 2005.

Huxley, Anthony. *The Painted Garden: The Garden through the Artist's Eye.* The Wellfleet Press: Wellfleet, MA, 1988.

Munroe, Enid. *An Artist in the Garden: A Guide to Creative and Natural Gardening.* Henry Holt & Company: New York, 1994.

Nollman, Jim. *Why We Garden: Cultivating a Sense of Place.* Sentient Publications: Boulder, CO, 2005.

### CDs about Artists and How They Lived and Worked

Clouzot, Henri-Georges. *The Mystery of Picasso,* with cinematography by Claude Renoir, originally filmed in 1955 and available from Netflix.

Cox, Paul. *The Life and Death of Vincent Van Gogh,* 1988. Available from Netflix.

Evans, Kim. *Marc Chagall,* 1985, available from Netflix.

Schmid, Richard. *Richard Schmid Paints the Landscape—June.* Stove Prairie Press, Richard-Schmid.com.

Schmid, Richard. *Richard Schmid Paints the Landscape— November.* Stove Prairie Press, Richard-Schmid.com.

Schmid, Richard. *Richard Schmid, The Capital Collection— Retrospective Works.* Stove Prairie Press, RichardSchmid.com.

### Miscellaneous

Garmey, Jane. *The Writer in the Garden.* Algonquin Books: Chapel Hill, NC, 1999.

Smith, Alexander McCall. *In the Company of Cheerful Ladies.* First Anchor Books: New York, 2004.

Tuan, Yi-Fu. *Space and Place: The Perspective of Experience.* University of Minnesota Press: Minneapolis, 1977.

Wheeler, David, editor. *The Penguin Book of Garden Writing.* Penguin Books: London, 1996.

# Index

## A

Abrams, Lucien, 118, 122
abstract expressionism, 38–41, 42
abstract expressionist gardens: description of, 38–41; comparison to abstract expressionist painting, 40
abstract expressionists, 38
*Acer triflorum*, 113
*Aconitum carmichaelii* 'Barker's Variety', 134
*Aconitum napellus*, 42
*Agapanthus* sp., 160
*Agapanthus* spp., 160
"A Gentle Plea for Chaos," 22
*Ajuga reptans* 'Atropurpurea', 134
*Alchemilla mollis*, 93, 134–35
*Alla Prima* (book), 70
*alla prima* (painting style), 69
*Allium aflatunense*, 45, 134
*Allium christophii*, 135
American Society of Portrait Artists, 69
*Anemone blanda*, 134
*Anemone vitifolia* 'Robustissima', 135
Anthony Mitchell Paintings, 66
Antoinette, Marie, 160
*Arch of Nero, The*, 13, **20**
Arnold Arboretum, 69
Arp, Jean Hans, 98
arriving at the front door, 56–57
*Art in Bloom* (book), 160
Art in Bloom (museum lecture series), 159–61
Art Institute of Chicago, 56
*Art of Planting*, 101
art, definition of, 11
*Artemisia alba* 'Canescens', 135
*Astilbe* x *arendsii*, 160
*At the Florist*, **68**, **79**
author's garden, **16**, **25**, **29**, **103**, **111**, **115**, **123**, **137**, **139**
*Autumn Trees and Vista*, **76**
*Autumn, the Grape Harvest*, **136**

## B

Barnes Foundation, 67
Barragan, Luis, 34
Baselitz, George, 46
Bazille, Frederic, 27, 64, 151
*Bedroom (Le Boudoir), The*, 13, **146**–47
Beedle, John, 41
Bellevue Botanical Gardens, The, **145**
Berry-Hill Gallery, 47
Birney, William Verplanck, 58–59
Birren, Joseph Pierre, 11, 92
*Blue Balcony*, 67
Bocchi, Amedeo, 88, 144
*Bold Visions for the Garden*, 129
Bolotowsky, Ilya, 39
Bonnard, Eugene, 60
Bonnard, Marthe, 60
Bonnard, Pierre, 12–14, 52–53, 56, 60–62, 67, 136
Boudin, Eugène, 64, 151
Bradley-Hole, Christopher, 34
Braque, Georges, 30, 32, 152
*Bridge Over a Pond*, 12, **104**
Browne, Matilda, 12, 53, 56–57
*Brunnera macrophylla* 'Jack Frost', 135
Buscot Park, 80, **93**
Bussolini, Karen, 134, **143**

## C

Cage, John, 38
Caillebotte, Gustave, 27
*Campsis radicans*, 134
*Caragana arborescens* 'Pendula', 80
Cassatt, Mary, 27, 160–61
Cézanne, Paul, 12, 30, 50, 54–55, 57, 62, 78, 83, 104–5
Chadwick, William, 120–21
Chase, William Merritt, 67
Chasse, Patrick, **125**
*Chestnut Trees and Farmhouse of Jas de Bouffan*, 12, **55**, 83
Chevreul, Michel Eugène, 152
Chicago, Judy, 46
*Child in His Garden with His Little Horse and Cart*, 67
Choosing a style, 17–51
Chrysler Museum, 47
Church, Thomas, 112
*Cimicifuga ramose* 'Hillside Black Beauty', 135
*Cladrastis kentukea*, 113
*Clark Voorhees House*, 12, **57**
classical axial design gardens: description of, 22–25; comparison to classic axial design painting, 24
classical axial design, 22–25

Claude Monet Foundation, 155

*Clematis* x *jackmanii*, 134

Cole, Thomas, 13, 20

color harmony or contrast: 129; The Gardener's Color Wheel, 130–31; color schemes for the garden, 133; the vocabulary of color, 133; the power of white, 133–34; green: keeper of the peace, 134; grays and gray greens, 134; contrasting colors in the garden, 134; harmonious colors in the garden, 135; color combinations, 136–49

color in gardens: 129; The Gardener's Color Wheel, 130–31; color schemes for the garden, 133; the vocabulary of color, 133; the power of white, 133–34; green: keeper of the peace, 134; grays and gray greens, 134; contrasting colors in the garden, 134; harmonious colors in the garden, 135; color combinations, 136–49

color schemes for the garden, 133

color, the vocabulary of: warm, 133; cool, 133; primary, 133; secondary, 133; in-between, 133; hue, 133; tint, 133; tone, 133; shade, 133

colors, contrasting: blue and orange, 134; yellow and violet, 134; red and green

colors, harmonious: 135

colors: white, 133; white, 133–34; green, 134; grays and gray greens, 134; blue and orange, 134; yellow and violet, 134; red and green, 134; chartreuse, orange, white, and yellow with shadows for black, 136–37; blue, orange, and yellow, 138–39; yellow, red, and salmon pink, 140–41; blue, red, and gray, 142–43; purple, orange, yellow, green, and dots of pink and red, 144–45; pastels in gray, blue, and pink, 146–47; red, green, yellow, orange, white, and purple, 148–49

*Colour Schemes for the Flower Garden,* 152

*Composition of Outdoor Painting,* 81

composition, elements of: 10; primary path, 70; clarify the destination for the primary path, 70–71; establish secondary paths, 71–72; keep shapes simple, 72; the main point of interest, 73–74; the strength of open space, 74; looking up—strength in the unexpected, 74; creating unity among disparate elements, 74–75; overall structure, 75; the central focus, 76; overlap objects to establish depth, 76–77; objects with personal associations, 77; overarching idea, 77; Sweetland's sequence in composing *Autumn Trees and Vista*, 77–79; overall

structure: horizontal bands, vertical accents, 79–80; inner structure, visual center, 80; unity through color, 80; S-curve, 70–72, **81**, 96, 120; circle, **82**; radiating lines, **82–83**; group mass, 83–**84**; tunnel, 84–**85**; pattern, 84–**85**; balance and scale, **86**; three spot, 86–**87**; single interest, **87**–88 triangle, **88**–89

composition, overall: the process, 69–72; the parts of a whole painting, a whole garden, 73–80; ten methods of composition for the landscape painter and garden designer, 81–89

Constable, John, 90, 152

contemporary gardens: description of, 46–49; comparison to contemporary painting, 48

contemporary, 46–49

*Coreopsis tinctoria,* 44

*Coreopsis verticillata* 'Moonbeam', 135

Corot, Jean Baptiste Camille, 102

Cosola, Demetrio, 67

*Cottage and a Heart, A,* 66

*Country Life with Cows,* 42

Courtauld Institute of Art Gallery, 67

*Crocosmia* 'Lucifer', 134

*Crocosmia* x *crocosmiiflora* 'Solfaterre', 135

Crowe, Sylvia, 101

cubism, 30–33, 42

cubist gardens: description of, 30–33; comparison to cubist painting, 32

cubists, 30–31

Cynthia  Reeves Contemporary Gallery, 46

Cynthia  Reeves Gallery, 47

## D

*Dahlia* 'Red Riding Hood', 134

Daubigny, Charles-François, 86, 118–19

de Kooning, Willem, 38–39

de Nittis, Giuseppe, 66

Degas, Edgar, 160

*Dejeuner (Luncheon in the Artist's Garden at Giverny), Le,* 12, 64, 65–66

Delacroix, Eugene, 50

Delilles, Jacques, 68

*Delphinium elatum,* 160

*Delphinium grandiflorum* 'Blue Butterfly', 135

*Delphinium* x cv., 160

Denis, Maurice, 67

design principles: 10; straight paths, 92–93; the tunnel, 94–95; curving paths, 96–97; related curves, 98–99; light: dappled shade, 100–1; focal points, 102–3; man-made structures contrasting with plants, 104–5; the outlook, 106–7; contrasting textures and colors, 108–9; creating entrances, transitions, and edges, 110–11

*Dicentra spectabilis* 'Alba', 135

*Dining Room Overlooking the Garden (The Breakfast Room)*, **52, 61**

*Dogwood Blossoms (No. 1)*, 11–12, **14**, 86, **100**

Doncieux, Camille-Léonie, 152

*Douanier (The Dream), Le*, 13, **108**

Dufy, Raoul, 13, 138

DuMond, Frank Vincent, 54, 88, 110–11

Dunbar, Mathew, 155

Dupre, Julian, 56

**E**

Eakins, Thomas, 58

Eckbo, Garret, 30

Eddison, Sydney, 129–30, 132

*Elegant Silvers*, 134

*en plein air*, 27, 54, 64, 151

*English Flower Garden, The*, 152

*Entrée du Village de Voisins (Yvelines)*, 13, **24**, 89

*Eupatorium maculatum* 'Gateway', 135

*Euphorbia polychroma*, 129

*Eustoma* × *grandiflora*, 160

**F**

Farrand, Beatrix, 69

Fedje, Sjur, 159

Feininger, Lyonel, 51

Fell, Derek, 27

Finnish National Art Gallery, The, 67

Fitch, John Lee, 13, 84, 94, 124

*Flower Garden, The*, **153**

flowers, contrasting: *Crocosmia* 'Lucifer', 134; *Lobelia siphilitica*, 134; *Geum coccineum* 'Borisii', 134; *Aconitum carmichaelii* 'Barker's Variety', 134; *Helenium autumnale* 'Moerheim Beauty', 134; *Impatiens* 'Tango', 134; *Salvia* 'Indigo Spires', 134; *Lilium* 'Enchantment', 134; *Campsis radicans*, 134; *Ajuga reptans* 'Atropurpurea', 134; *Iris pallida* 'Variegata', 134; *Anemone blanda*, 134; *Primula veris*, 134; *Allium aflatunense*, 134; *Alchemilla mollis*, 134; *Salvia verticillata* 'Purple Rain', 134; *Rudbeckia hirta* 'Irish Eyes', 134; *Clematis* × *jackmanii*, 134; *Forsythia* 'Meadowlark', 134; *Tulipa* 'Queen of the Night', 134; *Dahlia* 'Red Riding Hood', 134

*Forsythia* 'Meadowlark', 134

Frankenthaler, Helen, 38

Fredericks, Janet, 81–89

Freer, Frederick, 56

French Academy, 26

*Front Hall, The*, **59**

futurism, 30

**G**

Galerie Berko, 66

Galleria Civica D'Arte Moderna e Contemporanea di Torino, 67

Galleria D'Arte Moderna, 66

*Galtonia candicans*, 135

garden and painting styles: romanticism, 18–21; classical axial design, 22–25; impressionism, 26–29; cubism, 30–33; minimalism, 34–37; abstract expressionism, 38–41; pattern and decoration, 42–45; contemporary, 46–49

garden as the setting for the house, 54–55

*Garden Bench, The*, 67

garden design by Patrick Chasse, **125**

*Garden Design Project for Beach House for Mr. and Mrs. Burton Tremaine, Santa Barbara, California*, **99**

*Garden Design*, 101

garden design, painting, and emotion, 50–51

garden designers, language shared by painters and, 10

*Garden Gate*, 67

*Garden in Haminanlathi*, 67

garden in the Berkshire Hills of Massachusetts, **117**

*Garden in Vaugirard*, 66

garden of Thyrza Whittemore, **147**

*Garden Scene in Brittany*, 67

garden, creating a, 11

garden, the relationship between house and: 53; garden as the setting for the house, 54–55; arriving at the front door, 56–57; view from the front door, 58–59; views from windows out into the garden, 60–61; a terrace relates inside to outside, 62–63; sitting in the garden, 64–65

garden, roles trees play in the: vertical trees in a horizontal landscape, 114–17; creating intimacy, 118–19; trees in winter, 120–21; the orchard and allée: lines of trees as structural elements, 122–23; low-pruned trees compress views under them, 124–25; positive and negative space, 126–27

*Garden, Summer*, 67

*Garden, The*, 152

*Gardener's Color Wheel, The:* 129–131; how to use, 132

*Gardener's Palette: Creating Color in the Garden, The,* 129

gardening, differences between painting and, 11

*Gardens Are for People,* 112

gardens, color in: 129; The Gardener's Color Wheel, 130–31; color schemes for the garden, 133; the vocabulary of color, 133; the power of white, 133–34; green: keeper of the peace, 134; grays and gray greens, 134; contrasting colors in the garden, 134; harmonious colors in the garden, 135; color combinations, 136–49

gardens, ways to look at paintings and: itinerary of the eye, 11; horizontal or vertical, 11–12; the vantage point, 12; man-made objects contrasted with natural forms, 12; open sky versus enclosed gardens, 12; mood, 13; contrasting forms, 13; scale, 13; visual centers, 13; balance, 13; temperature, 13; a sense of depth, 13–14; passages, 14

Garmey, Jane, 18, 22

Gaston, Henri, 66

*Gate of the Casbah,* 13, **142**

Gauguin, Paul, 66, 129, 140

*Gerbera jamesonii,* 160

*Geum coccineum* 'Borisii', 134

*Geum coccineum* 'Fire Lake', **145**

Giverny: 152–53; lily pond at, **150, 154**; Monet's house and garden at, **153**; Leslie Park at, 155–57

Goldsworthy, Andy, 16–17

*Gordon's Pears,* 12, 75

Grenville, Hugo, 13, 148

Gridley, Kate, 12, 74–77

Griswold, Florence, 53, 56, 58, 122

Griswold, Mac, 115

Guzik, Nancy, 69

**H**

Harris, Moses, 130

Hartlage, Richard, 129

*Harvest, The,* 13, 67, **138**

Hassam, Childe, 9, 28–29, 68, 75, 79–80, 113

Helen Woodward Garden, **107**

*Helenium autumnale* 'Moerheim Beauty', 134

*Helictotrichon sempervirens* 'Sapphire', 135

*Helter, Skelter,* **49**

*Hemerocallis* cv., 160

*Heuchera americana* 'Palace Passion', **145**

Heywood, Tony, 49

*Hilltop,* **8, 73**

Hoffman, Hans, 38, 82

Hoge Veleuwe Sculpture Garden, 86

Hood Museum, 47

Hoschede, Alice, 152

Hoschede, Ernest, 152

*Hydrangea macrophylla,* 160

**I**

*Iberis sempervirens,* 135

*Impatiens* 'Tango', 134

impressionism, 26–29, 64, 151

*Impressionist Garden, The,* 27

impressionist gardens: description of, 26–29; comparison to impressionist painting, 28

impressionists, 26–28, 30, 53, 58, 104

*In and Out of Philadelphia,* **48**

*In Familiar Surroundings,* 67

*In the Garden (Celia Thaxter in her Garden),* 9, **28**

*In the Garden,* 66

*In the Park,* 88, **144**

Industrial Revolution, 27, 151

Inness, George, 50

*Intimate Garden, The,* 10

*Iris pallida* 'Variegata', 134

*Iris sibirica,* 160

*Island Garden, An,* 113

**J**

Jamin, Leon, 66

Jas de Bouffan, 54

*Jason of the Argonauts,* **103**

Jekyll, Gertrude, 26, 45, 109, 152

John Singer Sargent Medal for Lifetime Achievement, 69

**K**

Kahn, Wolf, 38–39

Kelly, Ellsworth, 34, 46

Kiley, Dan, 30, 97

King, John, 66

Klee, Paul, 17–18, 160

Klimt, Gustav, 84, 124–25

Koons, Jeff, 46

Kreutzberger-Schwerdt garden, **109**

Kroller-Muller Museum, 67

Kropf, Joan: a design for a hillside garden, **97**

Kubota, Fujitaro, 90, 105

## L

Lacey, Stephen, 18, 23, 129
Ladd, Rosemary, 8, 73–74
*Landscape*, 86, **118**
*Large Drawing*, **98**
*Lathyrus vernus*, 135
Lauves, Les, 54
*Law of Simultaneous Color Contrast, The*, 152
Lawson, Andrew, 74
Lega, Silvestro, 66, 82, 106–7
Legion of Honor, 160
LeSidaner, Henri, 66
Leslie, Charles Robert, 67
Liebermann, Max, 67
Lila Wallace–Reader's Digest Artist-in-Residence Grant, 155
*Lilium* 'Enchantment', 134
*Lilium* sp., 160
*Lilium* x 'Casablanca', 160
Lillehammer Art Museum, 67
*Lily Pond*, **155**
Lin, Maya, 124
*Lobelia siphilitica*, 134
*Local Events*, **44**
Louvre, The, 54
*Luncheon in the Garden*, 66
*Luxembourg Garden, The*, 13, **96**
*Lysimachia nummularia* 'Aurea', 109

## M

*Maackia amurensis*, 113
Macke, Auguste, 67
Magritte, René, 10
Manet, Édouard, 27
Mangold, Robert, 34
*March Snow*, **120**
Marinot, Maurice, 66
Marx, Burle, 99
Mason, Alice Trumbull, 39
Mason, Emily, 13, 38–40
Matisse, Henri, 13, 96, 142, 146–48
McGourty, MaryAnne, 134
Mercer, Carol: garden design by, **101**
Metcalf, Willard Leroy, 11, 86, 100, 14
Metropolitan Museum of Art, 69
minimalism, 34–37
minimalist gardens: 74; description of, 34–37; comparison to minimalist painting, 36

minimalists, 34–35
Miro, Joan, 51
*Mistress of the Garden, The*, 82, **106**
*Modern American Gardens—Designed by James Rose*, 30
Mondrian, Piet, 34, 36–37, 39, 82
Monet, Claude: in reference to *Summer*, 13, 113; garden at Giverny, 27; in quote from Marcel Proust, 27; relationship of house to garden, 53; comments on *Le Dejeuner (Luncheon in the Artist's Garden at Giverny)*, 64; biographical information on, 64; *Le Dejeuner (Luncheon in the Artist's Garden at Giverny)*, 12, **65**–66; life, garden, and art, 150–57; *The Flower Garden*, **153**; *Water Lilies*, **154**; Claude Monet Foundation, 155
Moran, Thomas, 56
Morisot, Berthe, 27
Mosby, William B., 69
Motherwell, Robert, 51
Mount Cuba Gardens, 77, **119**
*Mrs. Whaley and Her Charleston Garden*, 15
Musée d'Art Moderne, 66
Musée des Beaux-Arts, 66
Musée Municipal, 66
Museo Civico, 66
Museum of Fine Arts, The, 9, 159

## N

Nabis, 60
Napoleon II, 151
National Academy of Design, the, 56
Nationalgalerie, Staatliche Museen zu Berlin, 66
*Natural System of Colours, The*, 130
*Nepata* 'Six Hills Giant', 45, **143**
New York Botanic Garden, 9–10
Nicholson, Harold, 18
*Nicotiana sylvestris*, 135
Nolet, Didier, 116–17
Nollman, Jim, 11
Northwest Garden Nursery, The, **128, 149, 149**
Ny Carlsberg Glyptotek, 66

## O

*Oenothera stricta* 'Sulphurea', 135
*Old Brooklyn Bridge*, 12, 83, **102**
Oldenburg, Claes, 86
Oliver, Alfred, 66
*Open Air Breakfast, The*, 67
*Orchard, The*, **122**
*Oxford English Dictionary*, 11

## P

*Paeonia* 'Claudia', 135

*Painter's Family in the Garden in Rue Carcel, The,* 66

*Panicum virgatum* 'Shenandoah', 135

*Papaver* 'Turkenlouis', **143**

*Papaver orientale* 'Helen Elizabeth', 135

*Park, The,* 84, **124**

Parke, Leslie, 153, 155–57

pattern and decoration gardens: description of 42–45; comparison to pattern and decoration painting, 44

pattern and decoration, 42–45

*Patty-Cake,* **161**

Paul, Anthony, 34, 37

Payne, Edgar, 81

*Persicaria bistorta* 'Superba', 135

*Physocarpus opulifolius* 'Diablo', 25

Picasso, Pablo, 30

Pinacoteca di Brera, 66

Pissarro, Camille, 13, 24, 50, 54, 73, 89, 111, 152, 160

Pollock, Jackson, 38–39

*Portrait of the Young Countess Schouvaloff,* **161**

Portrait Society of America, Gold Medal from the, 69

Powys Castle Garden, **141**

*Primula veris,* 134

Proust, Marcel, 8, 27

*Pulmonaria* 'Mawson's Blue', 135

Putney Painters, 69

## Q

*Quercus palustris,* 115

## R

Ream, Victoria Jane, 159

*Red Vineyard, The,* 50

relationship between house and garden, the: 53; garden as the setting for the house, 54–55; arriving at the front door, 56–57; view from the front door, 58–59; views from windows out into the garden, 60–61; a terrace relates inside to outside, 62–63; sitting in the garden, 64–65

Renoir, Pierre-Auguste, 27, 50, 64, 67, 151

Revolution, the, 160

*Rhododendron mucronulatum,* 29

*Road near L'Estaque,* **32**

*Road Workers in Saint Remy,* 11, 13, **126**

*Robinia pseudoacacia* 'Frisia', 93, 137

Robinson, William, 26, 152

*Romantic Garden, The,* 18

romantic gardens: description of, 18–19, **21**; comparison to romantic painting, 20

romaticism, 18–21

*Rosa* 'Robusta', **143**

*Rosa glauca,* 135

*Rosa* x 'Fantasy', 160

Rose, Graham, 18

Rose, James, 30–31, 33

Rothko, Mark, 38

Rousseau, Henri, 13, 108

*Rudbeckia hirta* 'Irish Eyes', 134

*Ruscus hypoglossum,* 160

*Russian Doll, The,* 13, 69–70, **71–72**, 81, **158**

Ryoan-ji Temple, 34

## S

Sackville-West, Vita, 18, 132

Salmagundi, 58

Salon, The, 56

*Salvia* 'Indigo Spires', 134

*Salvia* 'May Night', **143**

*Salvia nemorosa* 'Lubeca', 135

*Salvia verticillata* 'Purple Rain', 134–35

Sandes, Roger, 42–45

*Saponaria officinalis,* 160

Sargent, Charles Sprague, 69

Schmid, Richard, 13, 17, 24, 69–73, 75–76, 81, 158

*September Morning in Settignano,* 66

*Sidalcea* 'Elsie Heugh', 135

Signorini, Telemaco, 66

Sisley, Alfred, 27, 64, 151

Sissinghurst, 18

sitting in the garden, 64–65

Sitwell, Sir George, 124

*Snapping Trail,* **116**

Snow, Mark, 30

*Sorbus alnifolia,* 113

*Stachys byzantina* 'Helene Von Stein', **143**

*Stachys macrantha* 'Superba', 135

Stadtische Galeria, 67

Stan Hywet Gardens, Birch Allée at, 13, **95**

*Startling Jungle, The,* 23

Stella, Frank, 34, 46, 102–3

Stella, Joseph, 12, 83

*Stewartia pseudocamellia,* 113

Stewart-Smith, Tom, 45

*Still Life with Poppies, Orchid and Dutch Coffee Pot,* 13, **148**

Stufano, Marco Polo, 9–10
styles, garden: romanticism, 18–21; classical axial design, 22–25; impressionism, 26–29; cubism, 30–33; minimalism, 34–37; abstract expressionism, 38–41; pattern and decoration, 42–45; contemporary, 46–49
*Summer*, 13, **113**
surrealism, 30
Sweetland, Brian: 76; Sweetland's sequence in composing *Autumn Trees and Vista*, clouds, 77; horizon line, 78; base, the, 78; middle distance, the, 78; itinerary of the eye, 78, 82; point of it all, the, 78–79
*Syringa reticulata*, 113

**T**
*Table in Sunlight in the Garden*, 66
*Tea Party in the Garden, A*, 66
*Terrace at Vernon, The*, 13–14, 56, 62–**63**
terrace relates inside to outside, a, 62–63
*Terrace, The*, 66
Terrasse, Charles, 60
Thaxter, Celia, 9, **28**, 113
Thomas, Charles, 159
Thomas, Graham Stuart, 101
*Thuja occidentalis* 'Smaragd', 111
Toledo Museum of Art, 67
*Top of the Hill*, **110**
Toulouse-Lautrec, 60
Trafalgar Square, **36**
tree trunks, snow-covered, **121**
tree, oak: in a park in Marblehead, Massachusetts, **127**
trees in the garden: vertical trees in a horizontal landscape, 114–17; creating intimacy, 118–19; trees in winter, 120–21; the orchard and allée: lines of trees as structural elements, 122–23; low-pruned trees compress views under them, 124–25; positive and negative space, 126–27
*Trout Stream, Green River, Connecticut*, 13, 84, **94**
Trump, Doug, 46–48
Trump, Kathleen, 47
*Tulipa* 'Queen of the Night', 134
Turner, J. M. W., 152

**U**
*Until Just Then*, 13, **40**
*Upalong*, 11, **92**

**V**
van der Rohe, Mies, 34
van Gogh, Vincent, 11–13, 50, 126–28
VanWyck, Frederick, 56
Verey, Rosemary, 70, 80, 93
*Veronica* 'Crater Lake Blue', **143**
*Veronica gentianoides*, 135
*Veronica spicata* 'Red Fox', 135
*Viburnum dentatum* 'Blue Muffin', 76
*Viburnum plicatum* 'Shasta', 135
*Viburnum prunifolium*, 111
Victoria and Albert Museum, 67
Vietnam Veteran's Memorial, 124
view from the front door, 58–59
views from windows out into the garden, 60–61
Vigee-LeBrun, Marie Louise Elizabeth, 160–61
Villon, Jacques, 51
*Vinca minor*, 95
von Wright, Ferdinand, 67
Voorhees, Clark, 53, 56
Vuillard, Edouard, 18

**W**
*Water Lilies*, **154**
Wave Hill, 9
Welsh, Mary, 42
Werenskiold, Eric, 67
Werlin Garden, 30
Whaley, Emily, 15, 18
*Why We Garden*, 11
*Wild Garden, The*, 152
*Woman Reading in a Garden*, 66
*Woman Sewing in a Garden*, 66
*Women and a White Horse*, **140**
World War II, 38
*Writer in the Garden, The*, 18, 22
*Wyeth at Kuerners*, 74
Wyeth, Andrew, 51, 74

**Y**
*Your House, Your Garden*, 22

**Z**
Zola, Emile, 54